FIX FOR MISFITS
Superior Men Rejected to the Outside

**Theory and Illustrations
by Karen Kellock Ph.D.**

This is a new theory in psychology. According to Koestler, all landmark theories are presented in picture-strip format (right-left integration) to bring on the "aha" experience of the formula (the characteristic of all new paradigms).

FORMULA FOR THEORY:

**ALL SUCCESS ATTRACTION
ALL DISEASE OBSTRUCTION
ALL RECOVERY ELIMINATION**

The three obstructions are:
people, habit and food.

Remove your obstruction and
you snap to your goals,
waiting in the wings.

FIX FOR MISFITS

We didn't fit, we couldn't be "social" for it was trivial, petty, competitive, mean and global. By taking us out of context they ruined patriot pundits, banned as nuts.   It was like a big black cloud: Not being ourselves, not able to obtain, crying in the rain.   Since it was mental illness/demons, forget it--in the galaxy it's a pin prick.   Prepare to be creative: make yourself *apt* to receive the greatest. If aligned with God it's the Self He made. If aligned with self (and sin) it is folly and God evades.

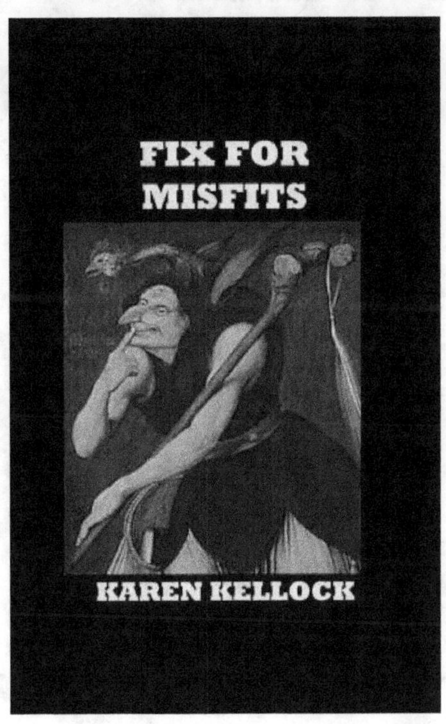

EMOTIONAL MISFITS

YOUR TIME WILL COME
BOUNDARIES NEED ENFORCEMENT
WAKING UP FROM ANOSOGNOSIA
DUNNING-KRUGER EFFECT
ENERGY VAMPIERS HANG AROUND
SIN SPREADS OUT IN CIRCLES
SEQUENTIALITY
TRIANGULATION
NARCISSIST MOTHER
REMOVE HIM/ALL HIS ASSOCIATIONS
SIN BLOCKS CREATIVITY
SICK SYSTEMS = SIBLING RIVALRY
ENERGY VAMPIRES
BE GRATEFUL FOR A GOOD HUSBAND
NARCISSISTIC TRIANGULATION
EMPATHS ARE HONEST
FREEDOM VS. TRAPPED
WHEN NO LONGER ENMESHED
NEVER MOVE IN WITH A MAN
WHO YOU HAVE TO BE WITH HIM
YOUR GUT IS AN ALARM BELL
GUT IS THE SECOND BRAIN
LIBERAL BULLIES FROM THE SIXTIES
WHEN YOU'RE MOST VULNERABLE
COMPLETION ATTRACTS MILLIONS

EMOTIONAL MISFITS

YOUR TIME WILL COME

Your victory may not come overnight but it always will because truth ALWAYS overcomes lies.

So what if he naps all day. If he pays your bills, solves problems and runs your errands it's ALL OK.

I will never love anyone unconditionally again after what I went thru with Jim: it was bedlam.

The truth is your sister's a serial bully and sadistic mocker in collusion with mom, a drunkard.

Not having confidence we work extra hard to be liked and have severe boundary issues, yikes.

You were mistreated in your season of treason but having repented it never happens again.

BOUNDARIES NEED ENFORCEMENT

Boundaries are not about what we request but what we enforce. Recall: narcissists bust them first.

Boundaries are about what we're gonna do: If you do X, I will do Y. If this isn't true you're done, aye.

Sin brings terrible reactions from family, friends and anyone else but it all ends with repentance.

When you recall your sin you'll remember the wider universe which erupted over and again.

WAKING UP FROM ANOSOGNOSIA

EMOTIONAL MISFITS

There was a lot wrong with me but I couldn't see it. That's called ANOSOGNOSIA of the addict.

I woke up to blind spots gradually and that's the past time of the elderly as gems emerge steadily.

I shudder looking back at what coulda happened with such bad company in fact. God saved a queen, alas.

After rescue God put me on the Potter's wheel for I had much to learn resisting people and their evil.

DUNNING-KRUGER EFFECT

Who gets attention in existence? The puerile, the fatuous, the inane, the bizarre and the twisted.

It was the Dunning-Kruger effect of having to adapt to dumb people. It's a frightening loss of control.

Ph.D. advisor warned [and pitied] me for trusting everybody when most won't understand me see.

With age I see the dangers of people and my narrow escapes: surely only God rescued me from evil.

Past persecutors may not even remember it since we swim in muddy waters and are blind to it.

ENERGY VAMPIERS HANG AROUND

Energy vampires are parasites: they wanna hang around to cause you misery for their supply.

Why would you want this? In a good marriage every day's a holiday/every meal's a banquet sis.

A charismatic vampire who thrives while you're in pain will cause you misery beyond evil dreams.

EMOTIONAL MISFITS

He even feels great about drastically shifting your emotions from joy to sadness--what an ass.

He needs to be in constant control, that's the point. In a split second he's suddenly out of joint.

I'm so glad to be outa this system when I always had to hide my happiness knowing he'd sabotage it.

I was blissful when alone--on top of the world--then suddenly thrown in with strangers/mean girls.

He thought he killed your spirit for good until he saw your picture, understood--and DIED the hood.

Don't go over the events God rescued you from. Rid PTSD by seeing only God not that ruffian.

SIN SPREADS OUT IN CIRCLES

The evil of sin spreads in concentric circles but with repentance the energy comes back into miracles.

You must remove value from the narcissist. Where you used to focus put that on you instead sis.

Don't blame them blame sin, for it's inevitable others turn against a sinner in compensation.

People take advantage when we act too fast in relationships. Move slowly and easily quit.

Making right choices while still hurting is maturity and is the opposite to vindictive treachery.

Seeing the predictable circle around sin allows you to forgive [the reactions of] family and friends.

Real world success is like a Tsunami: it feels empty or disappears at first then there's a giant burst.

EMOTIONAL MISFITS

Either you're an anti-new world order populist or you're a globalist suckup and they are opposites.

SEQUENTIALITY

Sequentiality: things in proper sequence. I had to be carnivore then God gave me my allowance.

It's called Sequentiality: things in proper sequence. You do things first then proceed to success.

Eliminating people is a great art that will bring you endless benefits and abundance: a cart.

Look back: all major obstacles were from people. Most losses were blocked creativity by evil.

Things are so much better when you go no contact, block them and remove all associations.

TRIANGULATION

With conflict the narcissist uses the dirty tactic of triangulation: talking to a third person.

He wants to control you and then control how others think about you--a very dangerous stew.

He wants to punish you and involve others in the process. Triangulation: what a mess.

It's comparative: the gang up gives message that you're inferior to the allies and their narrative.

It elevates him if others think poorly of you so getting that collusion together is top priority.

Majority fools? The dirty part is caving in to the "majority" rather than staying individual.

EMOTIONAL MISFITS

Psalms speaks of winning despite 10,000s against thee. That's the godly attitude to have see.

He doesn't care about anything but winning over you, so arranges a posse to put forth the screws.

Sometimes the narc's deep hunger for power and influence supersedes decency/kindness.

Mere disagreement he takes as rejection ok, so you must be punished and shown the better way

NARCISSIST MOTHER

The narcissist mother treats you like a nuisance and a burden she can't get rid of. It's cold love.

She puts your nervous system in shock never-ending and never soothes you when you're crying.

Having such a mother it's time to heal core wounds and a nervous system on fire since conception.

What causes constant shock to the nervous system? It's his emotional absence ma'am.

The narcissist is a grass-is-greener type person so once he gets you he then starts girl-lookin'.

Both the lovebombing and hoover feels so sincere but he's just getting you under control dear.

Once you buy the fairytale they start to devalue and falsely compare you as self-esteem fails.

REMOVE HIM/ALL HIS ASSOCIATIONS

Once you see the narc you remove him and all flying monkeys associated with him: new visions!

EMOTIONAL MISFITS

You must learn the words and terms referring to the narcissist abuse cycle, then you're free girl.

Dysfunctional family systems always affect the siblings like when favored child bullies one see.

It leaves an impact on sibling relations and deeply wounds the individual target like you son.

The traumatized family system shows scapegoating, triangulation, mom pitting one against one.

What child will listen to her, succumb to guilt trips and create supply? That's her favorite girl/guy.

So gross rubbish makes it big. Don't respond with envy, your time is coming-- for excellence not sick.

SIN BLOCKS CREATIVITY

SIN blocks creativity: need a moral revolution for renaissance or stay pat, boring irrelevance.

Children raised to feel like an obligation or burden feel they are of no value and it deeply wounds.

A narcissistic mom will pit her favored child against the nonconforming empath in hurtful wrath.

Mom and golden child become a team against the one, usually an empath who sees through the fun.

Happy when alone, suddenly I was thrown into the world of unfair comparisons and I fell down.

SICK SYSTEMS = SIBLING RIVALRY

Growing up in a sick system with sibling rivalry is the hell you gotta get thru to start healing too.

EMOTIONAL MISFITS

Narcissists doesn't wanna see you happy as they wanna control what, when and how you feel see.

Anytime you're excited about anything they try to destroy it. With success they kill your cat.

Your happiness burns the narcissist inside out--think about that sis for he's a demon and louse.

When you're happy he perceives it as loss of control and a DEFEAT. He goes to war and he's mean.

He tries to drastically shift your emotional state and focus back on him: now things get grim.

ENERGY VAMPIRES

They are energy vampires, thriving only when you're in pain. They cause that pain, over and again.

You had to experience war to set boundaries or to even see them as necessary. Be thankful for it see.

They wanna make sure you're NEVER happy. It destroys them: how Satan comes thru personality.

To actually perceive your happiness as their defeat: imagine the damage they do my sweet.

To cure your PTSD, be grateful for your war. It gave you social muscle , now you're the greatest ever.

BE GRATEFUL FOR A GOOD HUSBAND

Be happy if you have a good husband and give up greener pastures or you'll pay big time.

Does he pay the bills, solve problems and run errands? Then you got it made girl, stop complainin'.

EMOTIONAL MISFITS

If your man takes care of business in the daily grit of life then you have it made! Now no complaints.

Whenever on the verge of a new level, negative seeds come in to take root and destroy the whole.

Don't let that man in to plant negative seeds. Your success is his death and that's the truth see.

He seeks professions where he has power, can run wild without accounting and get multiple supplies.

Before completion you'll always meet a Saul trying to defeat your dreams but persevere that's all.

NARCISSISTIC TRIANGULATION

He'll actually groom other people to make you look foolish and honesty's not required sis.

Viewpoint-conformity makes a place unlivable. Enforcement is violent too: makes me sick as hell.

They suppress the truth and amplify lies. It's called calumny: wrecking your rep forever guys.

EMPATHS ARE HONEST

Empaths are honest. And this can create more enmity than you ever predicted: be subtle I suggest.

Truth is everything to us to be forced into a lie is ultimately a physical [disease] screw up.

They hated everything I said. It was as if their brittle fake wall splintered and they wanted me dead.

I'd been living in a completely different zone called the Family Myth. Empaths wake up/find bliss.

FREEDOM VS. TRAPPED

EMOTIONAL MISFITS

We want emotional and spiritual freedom and that wasn't it trapped in a scary/sick human system.

I had to be trapped in a couple scary/sticky human system situations to learn all about em.

Carrying secrets and lies we will get sick being empaths and it's always from other people, scuzz.

The family secret, the family myth or facade: all sick systems have hidden deceptions unresolved.

You're clear but suddenly aware of all the things you went thru getting here, and you're SCARED.

It scares me looking back because I see the great danger in maturity knowing the facts.

It is so daunting you come to the conclusion it HAD to be God who rescued you in a miracle above.

WHEN NO LONGER ENMESHED

No longer enmeshed, the family is unrecognizable to you now: strangers, aliens, mockers in a row.

Enmeshed in the system, a blind cog in the wheel, you didn't know them it was unconscious union.

No system is as cruel as one wishing to hold you bound. Be careful, find support, keep secrets now.

I edged out carefully. I found a rental, arranged a car, had bags packed and suddenly I was free.

That was my greatest lesson in psychology. How to outsmart a psychopath who'd kidnapped me.

For it was a kidnapping: I was so naive it was like taking candy from a baby but I learned real fast see.

EMOTIONAL MISFITS

NEVER MOVE IN WITH A MAN

Never move in with a man. Once in he'll kill the cat and make you his whore: a sad slave forevermore.

You move in with your husband, someone you can trust. Not these jokers: losers and temporary lust.

He lured me to his big fancy horse ranch and I stupidly let him fence me in with escape, no chance.

We're manipulated into situations when we're young and immature. Read these words/escape the lure.

An empath can't hold back tho' they know it'll cost the relationship. That's how important truth is.

WHO YOU HAVE TO BE WITH HIM

If in order to be in a relationship you have to be a liar, the empath cannot do that, it's torture.

Who I had to be in order to be in relationship was not who I am so I escaped/found a new man.

If I have to lie to hold a narcissist's fragile ego together that's a dangerous scene and bad weather.

If you still feel the wounds you're not an empowered empath yet. It divides energy on goals you set.

Forgive every sadist from the past, in order to be FREE of sad memories with which you reminisce.

YOUR GUT IS AN ALARM BELL

I had stomach aches daily. It wasn't IBS but my solar plexus warning me about the relationship see.

EMOTIONAL MISFITS

It was my **BODY** rejecting the relationship and it manifested in terror and gut ache torture.

This gut is your second brain, picking up on **ALL** of the information the brain missed ok.

The gut detects and sees things the conscious brain cannot. Ignore these red signals or you'll rot.

Things are subtle in the lovebombing stage but your gut kept sending you warning signals anyways.

Your loving protective gut is yelling "this person is not the right one for you" and you'd better listen Sue.

The gut yells "they are not your friend, they are your enemy and will cause you pain without end."

GUT IS THE SECOND BRAIN

The gut is your second brain, picking up on what your conscious brain cannot. Listen to it or rot.

It's the predator sitting next to you responsible for all your nervous diseases, there until he leaves.

The response to a predator is the alarm system going off in you. Ignore it and you're screwed.

A narcissist is a master manipulator while you're socialized to tune out signals: beware sister.

The body communicates with you early on in the narcissistic relationship: terror in the gut.

The body can heal itself and **WARNS** of the predator narcissist but the lovesick label that love sis.

LIBERAL BULLIES FROM THE SIXTIES

EMOTIONAL MISFITS

Liberals in the family BULLIED us into this way of thinking until we didn't think at all see.

When sis returned from Stanford she was dictatorial as we were bullied/made to agree to it all.

I was afraid of her, didn't know what to do. My whole worldview was reversed, it was so cruel.

She'd start yelling if we disagreed, something she learned in liberal college in the sixties.

She was in therapy, blaming mom for everything. Went on anti-depressants, it was all bull see.

Right when you need em the most their mask falls off cuz you were supply before, now you're not.

WHEN YOU'RE MOST VULNERABLE

Right when you're the most vulnerable the narcissist will betray you and show his true self.

You're diagnosed with terminal illness: he doesn't care about you only alternative supply for him sis.

Your only function was to become their supply. Now that you're ill you will NEVER see that guy.

He's missing when you're ill: he's running around with other people for the same function that's all.

The narcissist promises a dream but delivers a nightmare. Don't get hooked/avoid this affair.

"Eat your veggies" was another dangerous falsehood of the new age. Now we find they're dangerous.

Since cellulite is fat you lose it on carnivore diet. Adjustment period, wait a month, you'll see it.

EMOTIONAL MISFITS

The carnivore diet automatically includes intermittent fasting since you're never hungry it seems.

That's another fallacy: eat eat eat. eat breakfast, on and on. You eat when hungry only hon'.

The skinny show wrinkles from protein deficiency but will **NOT** if eating enough protein/FAT see.

COMPLETION ATTRACTS MILLIONS

With completion the kernel attracts millions. As created before birth but you did the assemblin'.

I wrote three pages a day for 15 years and that produced a masterpiece based on tears.

I could write a library of books on how people hold you down, in fact I have-- you see em on Amazon.

SOUL TIES AND LOST PURPOSE

DUNNING-KRUGER EFFECT
BE A LEGEND TO YOURSELF
SOUL TIES AND LOST PURPOSE
THEY CREEP INTO YOUR HOUSE
SOUL TIES AND SEARED CONSCIENCE
LIVING WITH THE DUMBED
CARNAL MINDED AND IMMATURE
CLEAVE TO SPOUSE
GODLESS MAN ROADMAP
TAMPERING WITH REPUTATIONS
THE UNDERTOW IS ALL SHE KNOWS
SETTLING TO CHANGE EM
THE PIMP MOVES
MAGNET TO MAGGOTS
HERO'S PATH IS THORNY AND ROUGH
NORMALIZING SIN/FALSE DOCTRINE
FALLEN HERO SYNDROME
WOMEN ARE CATTY
CEREBROTONIA: FEAR OF DISORDER

SOUL TIES AND LOST PURPOSE

DUNNING-KRUGER EFFECT

Proverb defined: A self-standing truism in 1-2 lines, not to be viewed in context for meaning, aye!

Due to the Dunning-Kruger Effect I had to keep my mouth shut: a muted/silenced elect.

Sinners feel internalized shame but since all is compensatory it comes out in pride parades.

You had to be beaten up psychologically to get to this place, flushing things out you had to face.

Not all men are dogs but most are. Not all women are dogs but most are. There, we're square.

BE A LEGEND TO YOURSELF

Be a legend to yourself [at first that may be enough] then add character and something to sell.

Why we self-despise: I saw myself as a grasshopper because I was that in their eyes.

If a theoretician you're heavily conceptual--to the normal mind, invisible--and thus ridiculed.

After all your work and discipline, YOU CAN'T FAIL. Chance favors a prepared mind/good girl.

The completion of a Creative Act on earth attracts pollination then you're in success/renowned.

SOUL TIES AND LOST PURPOSE

God doesn't want you uncertain/unhappy with ups and downs--it's not what He hath planned hon'.

Never fear when you see evil flourish like the olive tree for soon he's mowed down like weeds.

Whenever you feel less-than, see the SYSTEM. What seeds are sown/what has he been sayin'?

SOUL TIES AND LOST PURPOSE

Lost purpose: The time we waste running behind pseudo-relationships who couldn't care less.

As he loses control he appears a caricature, a cartoon. You worshipped him but he's now deplumed.

Back and forth, he'd cause you misery like you cannot imagine. Cut him out and take a vacation.

No one knows what they're doing and neither did we. We swim in muddy waters--its social psychology.

I study the holocaust cuz millions of lives were lost so I must since those killed can't tell us what.

Libs think they're right and virtuous and anything counter to that narrative is dangerous.

Living in a small desert town on the main drag was like being in prison: no protection from thugs.

Forgiving doesn't mean we must have a relationship with that person--it just takes US outa prison.

THEY CREEP INTO YOUR HOUSE

They creep into houses--they are "creeps". They WORM their way back in, louses and sick freaks.

SOUL TIES AND LOST PURPOSE

Born clear, we meet a system that awaits us. In mal-adapting we make a template/recreate it.

Don't get back/show up bad actors, they're just a mirage/archetype for lessons learned.

Unforgiveness puts us in prison, forgiveness sets us free: It's nothing to do with them you see.

He speaks brilliance then a false self takes over and it's all discarded and forgotten in a minute.

With a soul tie her body is home with her husband but her mind is on the other side of town.

Illicit relationships is the main way Satan ruins our talents, personality, lifestyle and destiny.

SOUL TIES AND SEARED CONSCIENCE

The longer one's in a soul tie relationship the more incapable he is of appreciating real love.

Her inner realm adapts to low settings and if she doesn't watch out she's permanently degraded.

Millions died in ditches or gas chambers. It was beyond anything a movie could portray or scare.

The reason you start things but don't finish is cuz it's the wrong thing: choose differently.

LIVING WITH THE DUMBED

How to explain smart to the dumb? You just gotta get along because violence is also their song.

She keeps thinking about this other guy--tho' she knows it's wrong--putting her home in jeopardy.

SOUL TIES AND LOST PURPOSE

They're not to display emotions so don't know how to handle em. Emotionally brittle, they die son.

My theory of healthy candy: it doesn't have to be bulky to keep you alive. Low bulk/high calorie.

He was a different person every time I saw him. I saw him as complex/at times wanted to kill him.

Abuse isn't even felt after adaptation. We've lost sensitivity, it doesn't hurt when put down.

The dumber they are the more they can't stand novelty so my stint in the desert was hard see.

Due to a seared conscience the more she's engaged in a soul tie the less she appreciates her guy.

Soul tie hunger is wasting one's days on a fantasy. That's how Satan distracts/binds you see.

A soul tie is an ILLUSION. Both sexes get caught and do nothing but think about that other person.

CARNAL MINDED AND IMMATURE

He's caught up in legs, hips and lips cuz he didn't pray for wife material. A loving future or a fall?

Many men are driven by their flesh, carnal-minded and immature, not having conquered the lure.

Once a man has a woman's body he is in her soul. The impact is totally different in guys vs. gals.

Emotionally and physically illicit sex is not the same game but both are judged equally by God ok.

Casual sex has a negative impact on her self-evaluation as it has caused humiliation for millennium.

SOUL TIES AND LOST PURPOSE

While the man is patted on the back as a hero the woman is ostracized: viva la difference, aye.

When a woman has sex outside of covenant she allows him to have free space in her soul man.

She is now tied to that man mentally, spiritually and physically and she's totally consumed see.

She's the only one who gets pregnant: while the man can disappear, she's tied to him forever.

Every sex event ties one spiritually, joining with the other's past sex experiences as well see.

A soul tie is an emotional knot prohibiting one from moving on romantically and psychologically.

CLEAVE TO SPOUSE

A woman is tied to her husband, the only one. The past they leave then to the spouse they cleave.

Marriages fail cuz there's a third party that one doesn't know about despite constant thoughts.

Soul tie flue: a third party is sleeping in their bed every night and spouse doesn't have a clue.

A woman having illicit sex is illegally joined but sex with her husband brings no shame/anointed.

Illicit sex exposes the woman's self-worth, self-definition and self-evaluation: BEDLAM.

The more she has casual sex the harder to see her virtue as she auto-ruins other lives too.

Something dies in a woman who's been toyed with thru lust. Call it maturity after this self-disgust.

SOUL TIES AND LOST PURPOSE

When played with sexually something dies in the soul of a woman especially with aging.

A history of mistakes from lacking proper instruction has made her think she's worth NOTHING.

She can't see herself being in a position of redemption increasingly weakened by men's pesterin'.

Illicit sex is not a loving experience. One just feels used: it's full of contradictions/questionings.

A soul tie can develop like a bee sting: suddenly. That's whatcha call magnetism/feels heavenly.

It's a lustful experience. And tampering with lusts always brings forth death, I can attest.

A woman over time with consecutive disappointments becomes hardened by the sex experience.

The wife of the alcoholic can't deal with his changes but to the others she's called the savage.

GODLESS MAN ROADMAP

A godless man creates a soul tie connection thru flattery to lower her defenses/then it's sex.

After flattery turns off her discernment he initiates a sexual relationship then rejects the twit.

The godless man hardens the soul tie by increasingly deeper levels of perversion til she's done.

This cad is always pushing her limits, bringing her into deeper levels never before experienced.

Via the use of perversion he's entrenching himself in the woman's soul and then she quickly grows old.

SOUL TIES AND LOST PURPOSE

She awakes to her predicament at times and tries to move on: right then her flesh yearns for him.

Her mind says GO, her spirit says FLEE but her flesh is CRAVING this godless little creep.

When relationships end men move on while women are broken. It's not the same re: the sex union.

Broken women in psych offices after being deceived by someone she thought she knew: whew.

Broken women are now stuck, unable to trust because the previous man played them thru lust.

He broke her spirit, invaded her soul and deceived her on the deepest levels and I was that girl sir.

Why do women get stuck and men move on? He tampered with her self-respect that's all.

TAMPERING WITH REPUTATIONS

Then he tampers with her reputation and sense of honor. Disrespect works to disempower.

When a woman's caught in adultery he tears her down but this isn't his function as a husband.

Her inability to accept total redemption--being washed clean of past sex experiences--keeps her down

Shame/guilt is the glue the enemy uses to maintain the soul tie for it dehumanizes the victim see.

I became desensitized--seared--by how cruel people were just to get through it but now I see it.

The wrong place is a nightmare ready to kill you, a snake striking outa the blue/home of demons too.

SOUL TIES AND LOST PURPOSE

Stop forcing your work. Your most productive times are looking out the window: take time off first.

True genius knows the value of leisure. Would-be genius has an incapacity for it for sure.

Since the best insights come in leisure [relaxation] a true genius does not exhibit workaholism.

Yet a genius may work like a surge for days and nights without stop, as creative action prompts.

There's nothing the blood of Jesus can't cleanse. And once He does your identity has changed.

As holy spirit enters evil spirits are denounced and evicted and she's no more zvengali-addicted.

The painful addiction to someone who hurts her is a thrill ride like any other adrenalin-trigger.

THE UNDERTOW IS ALL SHE KNOWS

The undertow like a moth to the flame is removed when she sees herself vis-a-vis this old game.

You are who God says you are: you are not your past. Once He cleanses you're in a NEW cast.

Don't let the world define you. Only God can define you and He says the past is white as snow too.

Every memory holding us in bondage is an anchor of Satan cuz he doesn't want us high/joyous.

I pray God breaks all chains for it is obstruction: "break every chain" is how you should be prayin'.

The wicked tie us up with bands. These subtle control devices are a severe undertow for women.

SOUL TIES AND LOST PURPOSE

When my hedge was blown I had no control over others and it was hell on earth, a spiraling down.

But adding sex to the mix equals a deeper hell: a massive soul tie for decades long spells.

God doesn't want us controlled by others and will always give an escape from such fakers.

God doesn't want illicit sex so will provide escape with the promise: the past is cleansed ok?

A big mistake is women thinking they can hook a husband with sex tho' her image is wrecked.

Having sex with a man she's not married to vastly diminishes his perception of her value.

There is no gender equality when it comes to sex. A nasty man is a player, a loose woman a hex.

She can't charge for hamburger and make him think it's steak. He can't make a wife out of a freak.

SETTLING TO CHANGE EM

A big mistake is settling for bad men to change em: trying to change a hobo like his mom couldn't.

How can we change a man's character who has none? He's just appetites processed one by one.

You can't change a fool cuz he's right in his own eyes. Must know: we can't change a fool's mind.

Women talk too much. A fool uttereth all his mind but a wise man keeps it in: shut your dam mouth.

Biggest mistake of girls: never take advice from women who are alone and angry with the world.

SOUL TIES AND LOST PURPOSE

Warning: many women lose good men from taking advice from females who don't have one.

Take advice from women who are happily married, not angry feminists who hate all men honey.

How friends annoy: walk with wise men and be wise, a companion of fools shall be destroyed.

If the blind lead the blind both fall into a ditch. The worst advice possible is from that witch.

We learn in life from instruction or experience. Listen or learn the hard way from this dalliance.

She's always reconciling the relationship even when he's wrong, a common theme on the begging end.

THE PIMP MOVES

The pimp move: He's never wrong/never apologizes so she must be the one to call so it resumes.

Just like a pimp on the street he creates a soul tie emotional addiction by never being wrong.

He beats her up/she apologizes to get him back. That's the system in a world so cold and black.

A nice girl never dated cuz mens expectations of sex on the first date was way too invasive.

A man with bad intentions doesn't like questions like what happened with prior affections.

MAGNET TO MAGGOTS

A broken female whose hedge is down is a magnet to maggots while being incapable of stopping it.

SOUL TIES AND LOST PURPOSE

I had to go thru pure bedlam, constant interruptions and dumbed invasions to understand ME my son.

I had to "let em all in" in order to change my life forever and vet every single person and friends.

The postwar social generation became careless when we were told to just be a good hostess.

For many people are bored and lonely so will drive you crazy until you learn to draw boundaries.

You will have many suitors. Ask questions to flush out their temperaments, are they avoiders?

Does he try to wave off a serious question? One of great import learned from past bedlam?

Healthy candy, I'm good for 24 hours and kitchen stays clean and orderly while I fast empowered.

If two BE AGREED: how can we have the same goals if we aren't walking the same walk see.

It's a hard, hard lesson and then as her self-esteem lessens she gets looser, needing more affection.

HERO'S PATH IS THORNY AND ROUGH

Hero's path: you must go thru humiliation [day of humbling] to get to elite rule in your kingdom.

The hero's path was thorny and rough but don't get PTSD over it, that's stupid and inefficient.

You were so sheltered/uninstructed you had to be hurt bad to pop out of it til now: you're perfect.

It won't repeat cuz you're totally protected whereas before you didn't even feel the need for it.

SOUL TIES AND LOST PURPOSE

My Ph.D. in the Streets was hard won learning more than a library of books about the scum.

Her husband is her covering. She doesn't share her heart with many words to any other man.

She will lose a good man by taking the advice of lonely angry women but that's how it's happenin'

People are cruel, I learned that the first day in school. Women belong at home not the human zoo.

NORMALIZING SIN/FALSE DOCTRINE

In trying to make their sin normal they suppress the truth of God and demonize their accusers all.

They make their own gods so they can do what they want and not violate their own principals.

I just wanna fast. Two cookies and I'm good for 24, then 36, then 48 hours between shortbreads.

I'm so glad to have eliminated all kitchen clutter and duties for 90 days of shortbread break-fasts.

Women stop spilling your brains on people. Wear a poker face/say nothing, that's good of you.

Harsh punishments: they don't convert people they conquer them--the tyrants and women.

Subhuman ass definition: a self-righteous slob in every situation not knowing anything, nouthin'.

Hero's Path: Savior archetype begins as subhuman ass. Overcoming ridicule: the ladder to success.

Success comes with finding the unique self and God who designed it. Now, it's any minute.

SOUL TIES AND LOST PURPOSE

Enantiodromia: everything converts to its opposite. Self-forgiveness is key/try to forget it.

I don't wanna meet up with anyone who knew me at 16. I shudder to think of it/too embarrassing.

Of course they're all dead who witnessed it and when I'm gone the memory's dissolved/the end.

FALLEN HERO SYNDROME

Fallen Hero Syndrome: He has no friends as he spirals down in fact they all wanna kill him.

Died in the gutter or became a famous orator? For these extremes there is no in-between.

We all have problems with memory. Addictions are devices to avoid em but they get worse see.

Anosognosia: can't see he's killing himself, like a giant blind spot--unaware of his condition/a nut.

I don't ever leave my home: that's where everything's at and I'm protected from dam dirty rats.

Dunning-Kruger is when the dumb rule and there's nothing you can do since they're blind too.

What is home? A building/set of routines while protected from the elements/unwanted people.

Having no instruction people get crooked when self-interest or appetites set in: don't let em.

WOMEN ARE CATTY

Women are catty behind the scenes and it's bitter and mean, reinforced by their smear campaigns.

SOUL TIES AND LOST PURPOSE

Once you're good they can't see the bad--can't view both sides of a gestalt simultaneously.

All sins are alike hon': Buried in the deepest ocean and then God puts up a sign: "don't go fishin'".

Music and looking out the window is more productive than stuffing yourself with videos/info.

She can always find reasons with a chip on her shoulder. Things are tranquil/then the bummer.

CEREBROTONIA: FEAR OF DISORDER

Cerebrotonia: fear of disorder and desire for privacy with trouble--that's me and my kennel.

You judge a person by their track record but liberal women won't do that: it's by their narrative.

To growth devotees: The world will be overwhelmingly pleased with your triumph of ideas.

For many years I couldn't overcome ridicule and was actually silenced: always on mute.

If patient the whole Creative Act together with the link itself will fall together in a fabric.

FIX FOR MISFITS

We didn't fit, we couldn't be "social" for it was trivial, petty, competitive, mean, sexual and global.

Prepare to be continuously creative. Make yourself apt to receive the greatest.

My work is done, now where is all the fun? I felt lost but music opened me up instantly, joy again.

If aligned with God you find the Self He made. If aligned with self (and in sin) it is folly/God evades.

Thank you God for this work You've given me to do. It's so amazing and fascinating to me too!

Creativity is what comes *through* you not something you have so just get clear and open the valve.

Creative work comes in spurts. You work, you relax. TV confuses things--too high a tax with dense facts.

You never know when the creative cue will hit: never adapt to TV time schedules or you'll not be legit.

All you gotta do is keep doing what you do best. It's like breathing or a bird singing IF you're unstressed.

Living in a tiny cabin in the desert wilderness made me appreciate rain on a tin roof: godliness.

Looking back it was like a big black cloud: Not being myself, not able to obtain, crying in the rain.

Since it was mental illness/demons, forget it. Get offa that thing, in the galaxy it's just a pin prick.

FIX FOR MISFITS

Marginal people go off like a rocket when incited by these maggots.

The tide has turned in America, the youth are pro-life. These big changes need to reflect gov on high.

Hollywood must stop it's violent rhetoric cuz that's really the impetus.

By taking them outa context they ruin the careers of patriot pundits: they are banned as nuts.

Left is embracing homicide as a political solution in their delusion.

Called the "god of light" Lucifer's actually the god of darkness: poverty, failure, lies, death and blight.

Obama's trying to get a race war going and they're already breaking into mansions. Baiting factions.

We all know he's a traitor now. But what of your friends and family still stuck in his delusions--wow!

There've been national saviors through history and we have one now but that doesn't stop the left's new lows.

Jon Stewart is a government jester. He's bought and paid for to lay eggs in you then let it all fester.

Bored with sex they only find solace (ecstasy) in mob violence

Diversity kills quality.

FIX FOR MISFITS

The Methodists have gone totally liberal. Was born/baptized in the church but this is a shame after all.

Demons in the pews.

Always go after power but pretend to care about morality. Saul Alinsky

Since progressives resented American superiority, kicking us down was their greatest priority.

Shaming of America: a progressive scheme to rip her off headed by Obama.

The radical left is communist, period. Very short-sighted but they too are the victims of this bad spirit.

The Great Uniter spent 8 years dividing people for political gain.

His army is armed and everywhere. Bombs and bullets--there are more of them than us, for sure.

In times of tyranny they hire low IQ's (dummies) to do the dirty work. We get nothing, they get perks.

Their plan: kill president, start civil war and Martial Law.

Another way they destroy is through confusion. On our most basic instincts they're creating de-evolution.

I knew the left was bad but to merge with a group who does those things--like Marquis de Sade?

The liberty movement is generating nuclear energy--we're all high. The left is destroyed, bye bye.

FIX FOR MISFITS

With knowledge comes great sorrow cuz we see the difference between God and the darkness below.

Chips-on-their-shoulder mental patients.

When self-love is lost evil power fills the vacuum: America stopped seeing itself as superior, doomed.

His father in Kenya or childhood in Indonesia--is more important than the greatness of America?

Cultural diversity doesn't always go smoothly. More often than not it causes great difficulty, truly.

We could go under total tyranny. We must face how we did it to ourselves, and see the strange irony.

Liberalism is about control--our founders were escaping this to establish rights, ya know.

The "affordable care act" triples prices, cuts quality care and rations it with death panels and cheap devices.

"Sustainable" is the sickest word. Whenever you hear it, turn away--it's the destruction of our world.

Despair or pessimism are common reactions to seeing corruption.

It's the democrats everywhere CALLING for a civil emergency--arrest, removal, death: suddenly.

Trump with our back: turning on economy/doing everything he said and they hate him for that.

FIX FOR MISFITS

Corny comedians playing to the biases and vanities of their audience, political prisoners of conformity.

She's the poster child for the arrogance of the left and the tombstone for liberalism: daft.

They dragged us down to avoid disapproval then things went too far so now we want their removal.

The William Morris Agency represents a terrorist and ISIS sympathizer.

Revitalization Movements are when the herd marches to a new beat-- awareness of cheats.

In Satan's world there is no justice: That's where the evil are honored and the good are mistrusted.

He ruined our great country and we let it happen. More interested in fashion/jokin we were nappin'.

The same leftists who deny the holocaust deny the monstrosities of ISIS. They see no evil nor crisis.

They wanna cause race war, riots, destabilization to blame on Trump.

Barry planned Martial Law for election day but Hillary got drunk and hysterical so he choked/went away.

Are we living in Trump's America or her reaction to Obama still, we don't know.

Good luck, you collaborators: The tables have turned and we're on top, no more censured and stopped.

FIX FOR MISFITS

Liberal-global view is bland, false, illusory, dull, sadistic, sexualized and communist.

The left wears smiley faces--but look at their eyes. They're pure disguise and what about all those lies?

The liberals live in la-la land--but life has problems, get real. God helps us through them, that's all.

Whites ended slavery but like nazis the SJWs kill the whole street/blame the whole race/not legit.

The left wants to normalize evil--can you imagine that? Doesn't that show who they are: ingrates and brats?

They cover up for evils of their handlers. They are gainsayers for gamblers-- they have no standards.

The backlash from GriffinISIS will only help us (the nice) in this crisis.

All these years you took the blame, victimized by leftist logic making you look bad--putting you in ill-fame.

Maoist tactics to defeat Trump and his agenda: Political warfare is a main component of this insurgency.

New fascism marches behind the banner of anti-fascism.

Video: Snoop dogg pushes gun control then assassinates trump with .357

The value of freedom is not known 'til it's lost. Boots on our neck is too high a cost (make that embossed).

FIX FOR MISFITS

Michelle wouldn't go with Barry to Arabia cuz she likes sleeveless tops and that's the scoop.

How liberals are bad: worrying about Russia but never Jihad.

Barry said "all nations are equal" meaning no American exceptionalism or guiding light—fool

No Barrack, all nations are not alike--some murder gays, women and Christians. Shame on you man.

Media isn't saying their swamping us with immigration but ask small towns across the nation.

The elites wanna conquer the planet to control it's fruits and that means you and me with no dispute.

We worship a new thing--the flag of modern Babylon. Prepare for death, starvation and vagabonds.

Most of the world's in tyranny--the default setting of mankind--where you lose your power and mind.

Not a word about ISIS just a bunch of other things. These are master planners and their underlings.

We've all been taught that fascism is a thing of the right. But it's the communist left, that's a lie.

Poland: no suicidal resettlement of illegals from incompatible cultures--only Europeans can now go there.

FIX FOR MISFITS

"we're as good as Americans, we'll show em". Thank Obama's speech, dangerous in what it unleashed.

Elevated himself to a healing God of the world while minimizing America and they all reflected it, ah.

The global tyrant preaches "diplomacy" first but that's ridiculous.

He can talk his way in or out of anything and that's how he gotten where he is, a political fink.

We want revenge against all those mockers who submitted our great nation to humiliation.

Remember, the fake will fail. Though appearing powerful now they'll deflate or go to jail.

Before I knew how to think I also virtue signaled constantly trying to get approval from finks.

Globalist flashy boy toy rulers talk so sweet like great humanitarians while we're up a creek.

Liberals love anyone who hates America no matter what they believe/can conceive.

Tyrants and murderers will always fail eventually, though they seem invincible, truly.

I'm proud of being anti-liberal (by choosing freedom and life) so all you leftists: skedaddle.

Is Hollywood more blackmailed or ignorant?

FIX FOR MISFITS

 **The whole world is a stage, each of us players upon it. Shakespeare**

Adapting to liberal thinking was the pit of hell but it brought out hidden talents/I came outa my shell.

Don't tell me we're all one man. There is good vs. evil, God vs. creation so protect innocent people.

Media terrorists want open borders, of course. Anti-Shariahs are called bigots in another farce.

Dishonorable trash reporting the "news", so out of line with the founders of America and without a clue.

Weak people grovel to the altar of evil. Despite your phony smile we the wise can see you traitorous people.

Theresa May's answer to terrorism: take all laptops but never make mass immigration stop.

We broke the back of the media monopoly. They'll now go bankrupt/sold off into the anals of history.

Fake news is unwatchable and not even vaguely entertaining--that's what happens when idiots are feigning.

Appalling, creepy, weird and totally unfunny.

Patriots are taking over the globalist power structure while the democrats are just regional, for sure.

They virtue signal of the necessity to take down our history and statues: way to fame for fools.

FIX FOR MISFITS

 **Bullied? Or just offended by criticism of Islam?**

Islam: one percent, Christian: 70%--disproportionate attention given?

Ramadan: Diligent to become more merciful to fellow Muslims and more severe against unbelievers.

The biggest qualm I have about feminism is it's link with Islam.

7 dead and 48 wounded in terror attack and London Mayor says there is "no reason to be alarmed!". POTUS

Great leaders are trained in pits or prisons. For me it was desert wilderness in a cabin giving joy and vision.

Crazy feminists don't know what they're talking about but if they persist joining Islam they'll soon find out.

How dare you find moral equivalence between my merciful Lord and killers instructed by their word.

They kill dogs you dummies. They aren't Americans who love decency but cruel invading armies.

About this hateful culture Trump said "I don't want em here". Blatant truths: that's why we call him dear.

These weak wimps take the opportunity to virtue signal, they're only claim to fame but obvious game.

They're so dense they can't see how horrible these people are. Denial, seared consciences, below par.

FIX FOR MISFITS

Liberals: You can't have open door immigration and not bring in terrorism.

Cultural suicide and insanity: lemmings. Never before have we seen national masochism/no condemning.

Communism/tyranny always begins by removing statues (history, tradition, grounding): please refuse!

Every jerk around is grabbing a microphone to virtue signal about how they hate slavery/it's fakery.

ISIS is internet media personality production houses and hacks encouraging lone wolves to attack.

Obama and Hillary hate the idea of making America great again cuz they are globalists, amen.

Border Laws: To protect the U.S. worker against unfair competition and to protect his life and health.

As the state becomes God everything else collapses. Family, culture and what we know as geniuses.

There's no such thing as "socialism". It's social engineers and elites controlling the money: rigged-ism.

It's so sick how they play on the public's ignorance. Socialism should only bring abhorrence!

They're just gonna let it happen? Yes, all this devastation is the elite's plan but for us our hopes are stolen.

When it comes to rioting social media has changed everything.

FIX FOR MISFITS

Change your diet then let your body morph. It's so exciting when of food addiction you've had enough.

Beauty may not be lasting but even in old age you can be flashing: eat right and there's little contrasting.

I'm inclined to eat breakfast and fast 18 hours from noon. I want all eating behind me, then I swoon.

If there's any fat on the frame, you're eating toxins because it sequesters into ugly bulges, in the main.

Stop eating everything that catches your fancy or you'll go dense and start to look ordinary (not a dandy).

No more orthorexia: I will now eat what I want, when I want and stay slender and gaunt.

If you ate too much the day before, thank God for now you gotta fast for the benefits you'll adore!

Middle age bulge doesn't have to happen. Just stick to real foods and eat once a day--it gladdens.

Getting your diet in order is the most important thing to (change your life totally so you can) dance and sing.

Diets become idols in those who embrace them. It's evil law or Christ to whom it's ok in God's kingdom.

We do not walk according to the flesh but the spirit. The law is the flesh (sin and death) and that's a diet.

FIX FOR MISFITS

Weaklings: there's only a few who can even diet. They have no resolve: they start the fast then they fry it.

Is he/she the reason you can't lose weight? Stress packs it on so unhook from evil and you will deflate.

Instead of doing the work, the lazy turn to gimmicks--none of which work whether diet pills or clinics.

"Lord remove my gut roll and make me a bean pole". That's all you gotta ask now just follow your soul.

As the body adapts to one meal a day, fat begins to melt away (it takes two weeks of this good habit, ok)

Habitual Daily Fasting: When the body knows it'll be fed, it burns fat (rather than storing it all instead).

The body sequesters toxins in fat so no matter what you can't get rid of that except to detox the crap.

Cacao in smoothie, great for morning errands. Wouldn't take it in the aft unless you want insomnia friends.

Just fast for a few days to achieve new reality, especially after faced with facts of a tragedy.

Bad memories (early trauma) are literally locked in sh*t. I hate to say it but look it up, it's legit.

Diets become idols, deceiving doctrines and lies in hypocrisy, ruling factors in lives of you and me.

Fasting: loose flesh gets tight and you're high as a kite when hungry at night.

FIX FOR MISFITS

 American progressivism: America stole all her wealth so hand it over pal.

Obama transferred status and power from the entrepreneurs to the resentful class of voters/gophers.

Since secularization it's feelings that guide everything but that's the devil and he pulls the strings.

To the left, logic is an enemy and truth a menace.

With Weiner's trial fresh and his sentence not yet started, it's alarming to see it all forgotten by the hardhearted.

It's only fighting for liberty which gives you magnetism and power: presto, opening like a flower.

There are warriors, collaborators and spies. In evil times it's a shifting alliance--everyone's in disguise.

Where's our force? Fighting for freedom's the animating contest which we're losing, of course.

Fighting for liberty is the animating contest bringing out our best. Start lecturing--that's the test.

They're gearing up and hunkering down--ready to take our liberties all around. Stand up, wear a crown.

Just cuz Trump broke the back of political correctness doesn't mean we're free, they still hate us.

Trump is still the underdog and they still demonize him cuz they're the scum who stole politics hon'.

FIX FOR MISFITS

Any victim of the little people would do best to turn it around and help others dealing with pests.

They abused her so much she preferred just a shack. This is Stockholm Syndrome, I had that knack.

The Fallen Hero Syndrome: when he starts to slip the whole gang pushes him more down, quick.

As suddenly as he rises up he spirals down: the shining star without the ground/never renowned.

No discipline in school = maniacs later = go to jail. That's what they want: we're set up to get fat and fail.

They get so bad (go so low) but when they've had enough of the dark side they become sweet/aglow.

One finds God then trustingly joins a church. Now he's got a brick to carry not a lamp to search.

What kills the churches is the spirit of compromise and control: let the world in and sell your soul.

When the churches show liberal characteristics and think they're good cuza them, forget em.

Compared to the world, America is heaven for minorities and women.

Engineering depts: Instead of aerodynamic lift and drag it's representation, feelings, micro-aggressions.

Decency, decency, decency not diversity

FIX FOR MISFITS

 What's it take? Daily assiduity. Day by day equals a masterpiece, truly.

What's it take: a sense of humor, a little lack of respect and you must work harder than anyone else.

Most important for your young genius is: learn how to handle people while standing high as a steeple.

The importance of an inner courtyard in nature secluded from neighbors.

Our mountain view: He would never admit that he was into the beauty, but how could he not be?

Stop trying to get it outa the computer and just look out at the view. What you're looking for is you.

To do your best work, simply outline the whole then fill it in when you feel like it. So easy and nifty, isn't it?

Just keep your work up. Stop confusing with all the latest, freshest or newest stuff that's really all fluff.

Always surveying the whole, just keep locking it into place then proceed to the next--like removing a hex.

Foolish consistency is always the problem. Don't fear experimentation lest the True Self be forgotten.

Our time is limited, we don't wanna waste a minute anymore

Tho' my time is almost run out I can say I've learned a lot and just gotta think back like a catalogue.

FIX FOR MISFITS

Liberals see jihadi fighters as justified pushing out the colonizers.

Kick America: undermine our allies and allow foes to gain strength--that's how Obama stank.

He thought we'd been stepping on the world so reduced our footprint: not cool.

Everything's secret with the left. The most draconian measures are signed at midnight--pure theft.

Moral collapse is not imminent--it's here. Just look around--we're a weak people ready to conquer.

Liberals don't object to gays thrown off roofs or women being stoned? They're on the phone, all is condoned.

We're now a lawless and poor republic. These are always run by brute force, you know it?

Most countries are in dark tyranny. America was a rare experiment--that we're losing it is a sad sentiment.

Nazis were socialists and Mussolini was Marxist.

Everything's about fake Islamophobia.

Islam, communism, sexualization and pedophilia: That's how they're blocking our victory.

Just another traitor/communist professor.

Globalism is bringing itself down. A bunch of billionaires wanting to make us all poor will be gone.

FIX FOR MISFITS

You just must do your own thing, for that is the highest most superior thing you could do--row or sing.

I gotta do what I do.

The saints choose beauty.

There is a tide in the affairs of men which, taken at the flood, leads to fortune. Omitted, life is shallow misery. Shakespeare

I can love you but still not want to hear all the details of your life. Shut up, please: listen and go lite.

Most memorable verse is: least possible words. Before he said a thing Einstein saw mental pictures.

Poetry can't be forced. It's only something that comes through the poet, then refined--that's the most.

You've been planting seeds: copy. So you know it's gonna happen, exploding open--yes not maybe.

At your maturity when they disparage, you don't have to say a thing: After a while they'll all perish.

Why I hate phones: it gives them a chance to abuse you with their garrulousness (their social-ness).

Facebook makes me feel loved. It says "good afternoon, Karen" and I finally feel so understood.

You get to your best and then you die. You don't decline but keep getting better then it's bye-bye.

FIX FOR MISFITS

 **Violent, hateful feminists marching for Sharia Law: please come God.**

Man behind the feminists: Soros gave 246 mil. for the marches.

Who hasn't been beat up by a feminist? Bullying scum: terrorists.

Anyone saying "kill Trump" should get SWAT-teamed today. It's a deep state coup d'etat as Trump purges CIA.

We hate em yet are forced to accept the normalization of absurd things but with God we're kings.

It's not true liberalism but authoritarianism, a front for world tyranny. They don't realize this currently.

Liberalism is the Tyranny of the Group. It's just like Nazi Germany and boy do they snoop.

Hillary calls retraining camps the "fun house". What can you expect from a duplicitous louse?

All colleges (except Christian) are left of center, meaning immorality across the board--do not enter.

The viscous liberal academics will get us all killed. An empty culture is a vacuum as fascism ful-fills.

It's a lonely life being a conservative nerd but all saints and geniuses are like this: the unpreferred.

The angry left is composed of conspiracy theories, fake history, name calling and language policing.

FIX FOR MISFITS

You must meet violence with violence, that is the problem. What's wrong is appeasement, amen.

The leftists have gone right to Saul Alinsky playbook and embraced it.

The censorship is ramping up where common sense is blocked

This savagery happened on our president's birthday. It was planned and will increase.

SJW's are about to reap the whirlwind.

If you can get past their initial argument you'll have millions of fans. Alex Jones

There is no debating that they lie. The fact we even discuss it shows morality has all but died.

The world situation is terrible but I marvel how it exactly reflects a culture that has lost its marbles.

Tyranny starts with things banned. Then comes the fines and prison times then death by the black hand.

We may as well face it: we've lost our country. Our history, traditions and heritage as freedom-babies.

At least wait till I say something before being offended. Ben Shapiro

They can lecture/castigate white males cuz they have moral superiority cuz they're not white males.

Filth outa Hollywood, garbage outa universities, hate from medias: we've had it up to here fellas.

FIX FOR MISFITS

Disrespect and French Revolution mentality after respect is lost. Ruin people's lives, get em fired, depose boss.

The good news is the enemy lives in palaces which are nightmare prisons, in fear God has risen.

Stop bringing invaders into your home and making your family adapt to em cuz you think it's good (scam).

Watch who you're around cuz by osmosis they're spirit is fed where angels fear to tread.

Learn the importance of an inner courtyard in privacy in sun/stars/nature secluded from the neighbors.

Synchronicity = it's your home man and it fits in history!

Learn to say "NO" and get your life back. "NO" is like turning a light on--getting gain after lack.

The world wants your "yes" when you'd rather stay home. Yes-men are miserable, amen?

If you stoop to their level they rule over you. In mal-adapting to their rejection you'll get sick too.

It's not you're a bad person cuz you needed approval, it's that weakness made wrong decisions for y'all.

It was like a curse that ended when it ended and nothing could be done about it (deserved it no doubt).

What you want to do is what God wants too. The world wants you to do it's thing then you're blue

FIX FOR MISFITS

They want him dead though he delivered on all he said and the economy's exploding, but they're red.

We could be flooded just like Merkel. It's all about what the deep state says is true.

Assassination mania is: desperation from unexpected Trump victory by dumbed down liberal minds.

They put politics before family/friends, and dissidents are banned/censured: these are the trends.

Those who love liberty are often alone--because conformists don't want our unique star shone.

Stop arguing with people who vehemently argue 2+ 2 = 5. There are millions of zombies alive.

There's either God or the devil. No lukewarm: You worship one or the other, so be very careful.

After speaking truth, rejection by family and friends shows you're smarter than them, it's proof.

I'm not going to lie about basic biology cuz it threatens your subjective sense of who you are.

What ridiculous standards: You must be a boy to be a boy scout.

Revelation: Men and women are totally different and facts don't care about your feelings.

Through "tolerance" we've become fruitless and dangerous as we let genocidal hordes in and we're silent.

FIX FOR MISFITS

It's constant sensuality: food and more food! I'd rather fast and be spiritual, happy and real.

It feels so good living in the moment when free of sensual desires keeping us dumbed down.

Food and sex are lower desires. By making gold--transmuting this energy--one can aspire/go higher.

Eat, now live in cosmic space: fast. Life above food's a blast, in a new cast doing divine tasks.

Less body, more spirit: As the body lessens the spirit grows--it's a way of being in the know and have glow.

Try some hip-huggers and you'll see the superfluity bunched up in the middle (hard to be slim as a fiddle).

The older model looks like Ghandi, not eye candy. He's not a fake trendy but sleek, thin and ruddy.

Eating too much is aging. You can see it in the gluttarian's face, sagging. Eat once: high-aiming.

You get to where you'll do anything for the look. The saints choose beauty or they feel forsook.

All those meals makes one fat and ferocious. I remember the bloat--not enough stability to be audacious.

Even with "good" food it's wrong to eat all day. Eat in a 4-6 hour window then fast: love life this way.

If one part tightens, the others will too. It's AUTOPHAGY: body excretes inferior cells through poo.

FIX FOR MISFITS

Anyone who said "kill Trump" should be SWAT-teamed TODAY.

False flags have started major wars and it's always government that creates this awful blood and gore.

"Must redistribute, all will be free, it's the capitalists stealing from you" and thus starts the killing spree.

They want a communist state as the elite at the top. Or did you think they too would be leveled off?

Need to arrest Jim Carrey and Kathy Griffin today

It's trendy to be always angry even though all psychological studies showing rages are pure inferiority.

You can't reason with the unenlightened. Block em and new life starts while you're still on top, fightin.

Immature men get grudges and these youth are the fighting force—can you imagine anything worse?

Don't forget: if they have no morals then they're also cruel. They don't care about you, they see you as a fool.

They say "I'm an intellectual, you're a racist (sexist)". Get smart—they're dumb as rats and accuse with out basis.

Calling whites "racists" works but cutting benefits to migrants means riots then politicians become clerks.

Bravery requires risk. Only now when it costs them nothing they hop on the bandwagon and enlist.

FIX FOR MISFITS

Progressivism is fueled by the most powerful human motives: envy, and they mobilize that greatly.

All churches can degenerate into falsehood, theatrics, effects and emotions: must keep pure doctrines.

You detest coming into contact with inferiority: the lack of ethics while demanding more money.

If Hillary had gotten in we'd be flooded with illegals suddenly and they'd come for the guns, really.

SICK of living under lawless leftist rule led by the cool creating feuds and treating patriots like fools.

Brits head to the polls to choose between a coward in denial or an accomplice to terror, her rival.

I must escape liberalism any way I can. Whether it's the girls on The View or all else they're into.

I used to be a liberal--can you believe that? I taught it in fact but then woke up about rats.

Historic events taking place. Our will is broken, finances destroyed, cajoled into total control, unemployed.

You take out our elected president and you'll see civil war like you never knew or heard of before.

You say Hillary's a good woman and I'm supposed to trust you?

The only thing standing between the globalists and total world domination is our little handguns.

FIX FOR MISFITS

Anywhere a Christian majority: prosperity, getting along, multiracial unity--doesn't exist anywhere else, truly.

It's not based on open society, creativity and freedom--only tyranny.

Leftism affects all in some way on some day--like suddenly having their kids/grandkids taken away.

"Offensive speech" on campus is having a non-liberal view--called haters, racists and bigots too.

They know they're wrong: To cover that up they act more that way, confirmed by the throng.

Get this: to question an accusation of racism is now "racist".

As the top becomes the bottom and the bottom the top the strange are given highest respect.

It's like a curse that lasts as long as it lasts then you come out of a dark dungeon and have a blast.

Block em then realize WHY you blocked em then grow way beyond em.

We've become so dumb there's no way we'll ever turn it around as we vote for fools unsound.

Pride themselves on how different they are yet they're all the same.

When freedom fails the best rot in filthy jails and those who appeased were hung by those they tried to please. Hiram Mann

No matter how sneaky he is or well-funded, if out of grace with God it'll always fail—Satan's reign has ended.

FIX FOR MISFITS

Merkel murdered her own culture.

Only a tiny minority are refugees--the vast majority are not/on the dole a lot.

Germany shows a 500% increase in migrant sex assaults in four years.

Because of those promoting unity we've never been more disunited.

We are witnessing the fall of Europe. They've reached a tipping point--the point of no return.

May news was 55% Russian collusion and 29 minutes on terror, questions?

Would you want a bunch of strangers coming into your house? Now you know how Obama's a louse.

Think of these fake news stations pushing that white man is racist and it's all about white privilege!

We hate fake news because they lie all the time, they push an agenda and they get caught.

Fake news is foreign enemies of the republic trying to overthrow the country and bankrupt the nation.

Global epidemic: fake news.

Hate-speech violations are leading up to anti-blasphemy laws pursuant to Sharia Law or anti-God.

Instead of truth about Islam, they name-call.

You've been threatened online for your life. Do you lie, cave in to strife or continue this great fight?

FIX FOR MISFITS

 **10,000 pedophiles arrested since Trump got in.**

Trump's pulling outa the TPP was our victory in spades.

Trump's pulling outa the Paris Accord ended the climate fight.

Trump: hundreds of Ms-13 arrests of those Obama let in knowingly.

The Obama regime will surely be seen as the most corrupt in the history of the United States.

7.5 million illegals voted--elections are rigged, dems doing it for years-- checkmate, Obama's chokin'.

What started an investigation into Russian collusion has now turned to Loretta Lynch. Obama unhinged!

Ban CNN from the Whitehouse press corp not just the back rows.

Blacks are only 13% of the population--Obama's was a white lib election.

A Marxist communist liberal progressive loves to transfer wealth as long as it's not theirs.

They wanna breed us out of existence in our own homelands.

Do you know these are the most barbarous, backward, evil people the world has ever seen?

Mankind is sliding, they look and act like baboons.

We ALL have evil memories and remorse due to deliberate demoralization by elite globalists.

Germans see their own destruction as an act of virtue and tolerance.

FIX FOR MISFITS

Find someone you resonate with, be faithful, live authentically and be cautious with other people.

Being a "player" or a slut is only a road to loneliness. Find that one = wholeness.

Men and women are meant to complement each other, it's our default biological setting and it's heaven.

From loving complementarity to war of the sexes from feminism's hatred of family (they hexed it).

Men and women must reject this manufactured reality, this incredibly harmful implanted tragedy.

Men suffer with divorce and many commit suicide. From ferocious feminists HIDE, in none confide.

Marriage is a divine institution between a man and a woman and that's a father and a mother, amen.

Watch out for old hippies, they've wrecked the countryside and the cities and it started in the sixties.

Media has fallen into the evil ditch. Millions of kids follow with demonic practices/being a witch.

America is a treacherous spouse who departed from a righteous husband who's now done, amen.

Won't stay on point, slippery as fish. Can't pin em down, virtue signaling, need escape (only wish!)

Oversocialized, we're more afraid to say something wrong.

FIX FOR MISFITS

Fasting, I'm not afraid of anything. Fasting, I'm joyous as my heart sings. Fasting, I'm the King.

The fast answers all problems. Be ready for the cameras: the breakfast-only plan for saints so glamorous.

Fast--and when hunger starts you know you're burning fat. What a wonderful feeling, I'm loving that.

Be like a snake as it all goes through. 24 hours and you'll have the new you-- you can see it's true.

Creepy, creepy evil clown. Wears a smile while we all fall down--MacDonalds though poison is big in town.

Snoop has lost his height-width ratio: he is square-faced, paunchy and looks ordinary/middle aged now.

Eat then don't eat. Enjoy the whole fasting day, don't cheat--then tomorrow beauty and strength of a fleet.

As long as I'm fasting, I'm queen. From breakfast to breakfast it's so spiritually sublime and freeing.

He who doesn't eat wins hands down. Eating lowers the head from the crown to an inferior like a clown.

Find a good buffet and pig out once a day. As you see the fat melt away you'll be saying hurray.

No more sticky spoon Chinese buffets. Yuk, I can do it much better myself with rice noodles and veggies.

Distract, haze: Diet/health programs is how Satan tries to destroy God's people in the latter days.

CULTURE CLASH BASHED

A Manufactured Clash for Cash

Live inside purpose, path is smooth. Rough path = popular groove. In a culture in rapid decline the left is openly invoking Satanism: very dark, old and twisted/not Americanism.   It's social engineering on a massive scale: leftist tyranny thru political correctness. When last Christian patriarch died the family swung hard left: totally daft as the social hypnotic depressed.   But we have the moral high ground:: on the right side of history while they go down. We want common sense of regular folks not socialists.

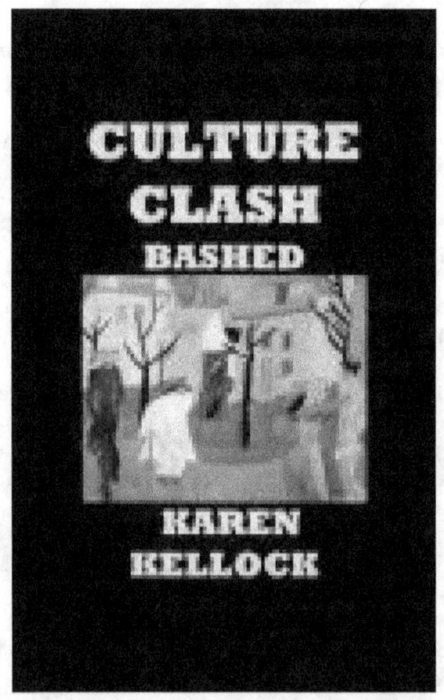

CULTURE CLASH BASHED
A Manufactured Clash for Cash

MANUFACTURED CLASH
THEY DON'T HAVE THE MORAL HIGHGROUND
DO NOT BE ASHAMED
OBAMA WAS THE TRAGIC "CLOSER"
FREE YOURSELF FROM POLITICAL CORRECTNESS
MEN PUT OFF BY NON-NURTURING FEMALES
FLU SHOTS ARE PACKED WITH CRAP
TRUE LIBERALISM IS:
WHAT DUMMIES COULD LOVE HILLARY?
MORE LOCAL, MORE SANE
WHAT IS INSANITY
BLATANT DOUBLE STANDARDS OF FEMINISTS
HAND IN HAND WITH MOBSTERS
HOW DARE YOU ADORE THEM
THERE'S MEN AND WOMEN, DOGS AND CATS
RAPPERS BASH TRUMP
WRONGSPEAK = OSTRACIZED FROM SOCIETY
STATISTICS ON GROUPS AND THEIR CRIMES
FEMINISTS CONFLATE LIKE IT'S "ALL" MEN
MANIPULATORS WITH THEIR OWN AGENDAS
IDENTITY POLITICS AND VIRTUE SIGNALING
THEY CRY WHEN ARCHETYPES DIE
POLITICAL PARADOXES
I DON'T LIKE LIBERALS: GO TO THE DEVIL
GO FORWARD—DON'T LOOK BACKWARD
YOU'RE THE BEST DESPITE THE POLLS
SELLING SOULS FOR A SLICE
WE DON'T NEED THE COOL
ALL IMBECILES CALL US RACIST
WIMPS CONTROLLED BY GROUPTHINK
DISCERN GOD'S TIMING: GO OR STAY
RECAP THOUGHTS ON LIES WE BOUGHT

CULTURE CLASH BASHED
A Manufactured Clash for Cash

Trump is amazing: the energy, stamina, focus, commitment and delivery is dazzling.

Trump demands fundamental fairness and blocks past hex (TPP) for America every time and for this, thanks.

We won, Trump got in, now don't worry about a thing.

MANUFACTURED CLASH

We're sick of political correctness and leftwing totalitarianism. We want common sense of regular folks, amen.

Big gov zealots, ideological fanatics and media promoting PC culture

As Americans feel increased prosperity and security, Trump will trounce the enemy.

As we prosper under Trump, the class/race warfare BS will be harder to sell.

Trump's epic and historic speech has split the dems: jump on bandwagon or face liberal abuse and chagrin?

Stole from the taxpayers and gave it to their pals.

Being powerful is like being a lady. If you have to tell people you are, you aren't. Margaret Thatcher

Crybullies on the left were shaken as they watched their globalist dream turn to ash/no more sellout cash.

Trump was an advocate for gay rights for 30 years before it was cool and he loves blacks and women too.

In a culture in rapid decline the left is openly invoking Satanism: very dark, old and twisted/not Americanism.

CULTURE CLASH BASHED

Satanism is only powerful against those who don't know what they're facing.

EPA is meant to shut industry down to put it in countries with no controls. To make America defunct, old.

Russian conspiracy: Neo-Macarthyist paranoia mixed with hysterical self-entitlement/supreme arrogance.

Stop caving to contrived leftist hysteria.

THEY DON'T HAVE THE MORAL HIGHGROUND

They don't have the moral high ground, but you're on the right side of history while they go down.

It's social engineering on a massive scale. Democrats are the best at this: liberals all tell tall tales.

I wasn't elected to spend my time with reporters and celebrities. D. Trump

Donald J Trump campaigned on speaking directly to Americans and that's exactly what he'll do.

Trump knew about the social tyranny/press-whores and sought to restore power to the individual once more.

Pelosi doesn't know basic facts. She's dumb as a rock and makes no attempt to educate herself, lax.

From trash to treasure in Jesus Christ.

Live inside purpose, path is smooth. Rough path = popular groove.

Liberals are the biggest fascists in the world and that's why they rejected you so forget about it little boy/girl.

They've already committed so many crimes they think they can do whatever they want, but not Trump.

It's become the Democrat Socialist Islamist Party USA.

CULTURE CLASH BASHED

When last Christian patriarch died the family swung hard left: totally daft as the social hypnotic depressed.

Survey: 98% of news coverage is anti-Trump.

As the pedophile arrests become massive God's people must fill the void of many openings as the brass leave.

If they don't wanna hear the message, move on. There's too many wounded who need it badly or they'll be gone.

Pastors who are not speaking out (e.g. for the unborn) will be silenced and you will see them no more.

DO NOT BE ASHAMED

I am not ashamed of the gospel of Jesus Christ for it is the power unto salvation. Romans 1:16

Hear Ye: Repent of SIN, symptoms leave. Repent of sin, symptoms leave. Repent of sin, symptoms leave.

The church took a bribe (501c3) and agreed to not talk the truth, so God's judgment will fall soon.

Church took a bribe to not talk about abortion and just look at the devolution.

Johnson Amendment: Pastors shut up when prayer left schools and when abortion became cool.

Disinherit the jerks. Jerry Lewis didn't leave a penny to his six liberal sons who never called him Sir.

Millennials think evil is good and good is evil, dark is light and light is dark, bitter' sweet/sweet's bitter.

Our Christian president is removing the Johnson Amendment so pastors can fearlessly speak again.

CULTURE CLASH BASHED

People won't donate if they can't write it off. So to get donations you get tax status by shutting your mouth.

Pray that God brings total exposure to pedogate and the true motivation of the Trump enemies/hate.

They are following their own corny script and God says "No, sorry--that's been denied" and then they're licked/they lie.

Obama presidency was a complete failure for democrats, he destroyed the dirty rats.

OBAMA WAS THE TRAGIC "CLOSER"

Obama was the tragic culmination of fifty years of liberalism then he did his own party in and I'm lovin it man.

Adapting to liberals was the dregs.
Obama's reappearance is like seeing a bad ex show up--irritation and "why?"

Obama doesn't get people elected he gets them defeated.

Obama did more to destroy the democratic party than the GOP could have hoped or planned: Thanks, man!

The bottom has fallen out of their whole reality. It's called the Ontologically Fatal Insight before insanity.

Purge is coming: massive pedophile arrests just for a start and this nemesis I'm loving after 8 years suffering.

Haha: the Democrats turn on Obama causing them so much trauma.

Trump gave 25 billion to black colleges, cut 2/3 regulations small business, stocks up 3 trillion: they don't tell us this.

A patriot saves his country from his government. Thomas Paine

This scandal is so massive and all-encompassing I just have to cut out and let the Donald president take care of it.

CULTURE CLASH BASHED

Facebook banning conservative pro-Trump news. Hello blues

It doesn't matter where they are: People through media are influenced by the same cultural neurosis--bizarre.

Undetectable assassinations like Michael Hastings where cars/planes blow up: that's CIA for decades nonstop.

Turned on FOX--no interest whatsoever. Endless details vary daily but I prefer being constantly clever.

FREE YOURSELF FROM POLITICAL CORRECTNESS

Breaking out of political correctness is the most freeing thing as you find yourself at odds with the whole mess.

Secret Service says Obama had 12 sex hookups a day. This stuff started in sixties: all about sex not "love"--ok?

Feminists maintain the right to kill their babies--this is "gains".

You have no right to bitch having it so good with white man in the west but you support Islam misogynists.

Phony feminists stand for "real family values"--deceivers! You should hear how they talk to husbands in secret.

Phony feminists want open borders--flooded with antithetical cultures. They're dumb as rats, female unthinkers.

"Better education for girls"--what about boys? We all know how the little boys are squelched, blocked, annoyed.

Discourse over gender became so nonsensical/removed from reality, rowdy resistance is unsurprising. Camille Paglia

They're sycophantic, phlegmatic and pusillanimous: soapy, stodgy and dim.

Older women are to educate the younger on morals. Not an old angry mean female resting on her laurels.

CULTURE CLASH BASHED

Borrego was filled with angry lesbians. This is not how it is--a blink in history, a deviation.

It's the birds and the bees. It is natural, it is God's will, it is a banquet and celebration, way to be pleased.

This fight ain't over about abortion/homosexuality just cuz you say it is. We say what God says and He's pizzed.

Angry lesbians scared me, they were mean. Borrowing "maleness" is unnatural, a perversion, a new reality unseen.

MEN PUT OFF BY NON-NURTURING FEMALES

Men put off by non-nurturing or displeasing females. Demanding, pugnacious self-involved witches, egotistical.

Why does Camille Paglia love "Housewives"? Boring, self-involved, petty, shallow, narcissistic, screaming/snide.

Herd is soapy, phony, stodgy and dim. Give up on em but still be friendly, that's just survival in this lion's den.

Because the opposition is mean we cave in. You have to be bold to go against the false premise which is dumb.

Feminist: Always virtue signaling and act disgusting. Shut up shallow female and stop your sinful lusting.

Concupiscence (tendency towards lust) is in all men and all men are sinners.

A lousy female housekeeper is shirking her duty. There's a natural division of labor and men bring in the booty.

It is an oxymoron to be a feminist or liberal Christian.

Both coasts are sick. But they seem to rule what it means to be cool so us bitter clingers are connected and thick.

Designed to take out the small healthcare clinics: a consolidation plan and screwjob by Paul Ryan, a gimmick.

CULTURE CLASH BASHED

Trump must have his own fireside chats to control the narrative, counter and bypass the blues from fake news.

Taking offense where none is intended.

Who rules determines when they come and get you.

They're putting cancer viruses in vaccines and there's white papers and patents on how they did it.

The cancer viruses go into the nerve and then activate later with stress. They aim to kill 99% of us, what a mess.

FLU SHOTS ARE PACKED WITH CRAP

Refuse flu shots packed with crap.

Starbucks' leftist stance gains nothing but a bash by the vast majority of conservatives in the world, at last.

How liberals think and begin to stink: Their false premise (anything goes) taken to absurd levels and over the brink.

Both coasts scare me--hotbeds of pomp and vanity.

Guns give you the right comportment: It's an evil world out there, not "good" as we were taught (to ensnare).

Maybe all your life you couldn't let them go, but they're liberals--that's all you need to know.

Liberals say "it's all good" and other bull. It's an evil world and we gotta be ready, draw lines, bring order, stay still.

Liberals are unprepared cuz it's all about social and that means merged together, unprotected and other bull.

Sorry liberals MLK believed in second amendment rights.

Patriotic red states like Utah are labeled "hostile", trigger gov claws.

CULTURE CLASH BASHED

We get to elect our president and he is honor bound to accept our will. Obama can't stand it and is here still.

Each time I see the red cliffs of Utah they look different. They are beautiful but best of all: not liberal.

Anarchists are anti-American socialists too uninformed to see how great they have it in the U.S.

TRUE LIBERALISM IS:

True liberalism: hospitality, low taxes, freedom, not judging. Modern liberals: obsessed, neurotic/unloving.

They fancy themselves intellectuals by mimicking silly slogans and sloganizing justifies their shenanigans.

Country folk: the nicest people ever, opposite to the obsessed trendies which are stormy weather.

The schools are actually having fake Trump assassinations and it's all from the liberal teacher's unions.

When nationalism exploded the dems tried to stop the tea party by calling it all "racist" (this was baseless).

Cut taxes, freeze spending and stop endless wars: We're there: total prosperity/innovation galore.

Trump is already presidential and delivering: Not on conquest economies but renaissance for you and me.

At first minorities shunned it but then saw the light on the tea party and now love it: we're in a new orbit!

What they call "fake news" is anything contradicting their leftist narrative: Jones, Drudge, Savage too.

They saw Hillary as more than a president but an idea, a world historical heroine, light itself. Haha

CULTURE CLASH BASHED

"Hillary is Athena" who can't be faulted, criticized or analyzed--all in the face of behavior we despised.

"Hillary didn't fail us, we failed her": As with all saints and prophets the problem is never them but us.

I disfriend liberals to make room for others able/willing to learn.

Hillary was "with out flaws": a peerless leader and benefactor of women and children: Mother Teresa in a pantsuit.

WHAT DUMMIES COULD LOVE HILLARY?

What dummies could make Hillary into a revered pope? Now you know all about your friends the dopes.

The female teachers are totally sexist against the boys. They have no fathers either/likely no toys.

Girls now feel superior to boys at age 4. It's ingrained and if it isn't seen as serious we've no future.

Female teachers give girls better grades than males, but if she doesn't know the sex, females get the fails.

What are his emotional/social skills, ability to get along with the other kids--assessing non-objective frills.

Bias against boys is perfectly acceptable in society. Teachers smile at girls but frown at boys/it's ugly.

Black-white achievement gap is large but the gender gap is three times larger/girls seen as smarter.

Now we see why men are checking out: cuz no one cares until the power goes out or we need repairs.

The gender gap in grades goes down one-third when teachers don't know the gender they're marking.

CULTURE CLASH BASHED

In reaction to sexist rejection boy gets rowdy in class and given an "F" in socialization/end of him.

Schools toxic for girls through vanity, and boys prejudice and despair.

Men are overly-apologetic about everything cuz they've been socialized that way in the school scene.

Truth: First it's ridiculed then violently opposed then accepted as self-evident: historical pattern, definite.

They hate Donald Trump more than Kim Jong Un and ISIS. It's a riddle and amazing state of psychosis.

MORE LOCAL, MORE SANE

More local, more sane--more like you. Here you get your own life back and what a relief: whew.

We've pulled the plug on the swamp now let's make sure it all drains out.

Generation Z is sick of hearing about gender studies, colonialism or the sin of being white, male or whatever.

Liberalism is an echo chamber and a default setting. We've all been tainted by it then wake up suddenly.

Most of the feds aren't bad people but they have special units of democrat scum bags, thoroughly evil.

How did we ever get to this ridiculous point? Creeping: an uninformed public slips into the wrong viewpoint.

Fake news talking heads aren't simply misinformed, they're complicit: taking payoffs, dirty, submissive.

Became part of the enemy through Stockholm Syndrome: an ego collapse then loving the oppression.

The media and education have been weaponized with anti-American rhetoric and it hurts when our kids speak it.

CULTURE CLASH BASHED

Liberals declare war on cotton and cornbread.

First feminists falsify a campus "rape culture" then ignore the real rapists flooding in like vultures.

How to run a household: to cook, clean, raise children well and participate in the neighborhood.

The How To Be a Good Wife skill set has vanished so what's left? Sex, but now it acts as a hex.

When women stopped housekeeping--when those skills were no longer handed down--men were leaving.

WHAT IS INSANITY

Insanity thinking: Wearing a black tent is liberating but a bikini is patriarchy.

Bone and muscle mass, stamina: all different in two genders, hah.

"Transphobic systemic violence" means: advancing the case of fixed binaries (male/female), the crime of "bio essentialism".

"Crime of genocide": describing the male/female divide.

Talk of chromosomes is censured out now by trendies who know.

"Chromosomes determine gender" deleted on Netflix: All of science has gone under, without a fix.

No more "I think therefore I am" but "I'm a victim therefore I am" and I don't exist without it man.

The insanity of the cultural revolution in 2017. Berkeley is crucial in history of free speech rights/education.

Universities: Free speech only for the left not conservatives, centrists or even centrist liberals.

College administrators are the problem, caving into this and also radical leftist faculty leading this.

CULTURE CLASH BASHED

Socialism always gives birth to poverty cuz that's the only way you can make sure of everyone's equality.

Socialism gives birth to poverty cuz that's the only way you can make sure of everyone's equality.

Communism is not swaddled infancy forever from hatred and fear of competition cuz it's all illusion.

Attack my politics attack my identity and that's my right to violence: the micro-aggression mentality.

In the Oppression Olympics the white man is at the bottom seen as rotten.

BLATANT DOUBLE STANDARDS OF FEMINISTS

"1 in 5 women raped on campus": LIE. Gang rapes across Europe: ignored by feminists, no outcry.

Trump: Like a light switch prosperity floods back in. Listen up Americans we've never had such a friend.

At anti-Trump demonstrations you can't find anyone who looks normal. These creatures are carnal, awful, immoral.

What they do against Trump fails cuz it's out of grace, not of God and Satanic--thus rappers do it.

They're twisted and bitter against the wholesome: loving families, concern, decency and religion forgotten.

Someone finds the Lord then goes to a church and is shocked by the difference and spiritually blocked.

Left is so blind, daft and dumb they loved Obama for his big smile alone.

Get that lizard out! Ban him, arrest him, deport him: end our drought.

Everything they say is glowing empty words. That's liberalism: a facade of goodness covering over turds.

CULTURE CLASH BASHED

Why should we give into stupidity just cuz it yells the loudest and fights in these absurd ways?

By a strange twist of mean fate Pelosi had to face the monsters she herself helped to create.

Haha. Hillary's been supporting Antifa. She's still calling the shots to uproot the deplorables of America.

We thought it was Soros behind it but no it's Hillary who refuses to give up but financing Antifa?

Real enemy of Atifa: average American citizen.

Defund UC (soon) until they discipline the domestic terrorists called Antifa and rent-a-mob goons.

HAND IN HAND WITH MOBSTERS

UC officials are in cahoots with Antifa violence. Defund the campuses or we haven't a chance.

How is Donald Trump a racist? CNN has told Black people he is and otherwise there's no basis.

Pelosi caught in her own web: How do you like confronted by ungrateful brats on the other end?

The most cowardly thing is to fall in with liberal Hollywood and say stupid things about Trump.

The Emmy's are like any trade show--e.g. garbage men giving each other awards. Michael Savage

Antifa-funder (mean witch) Hillary Clinton: look at their weapons coming against ordinary Americans.

Low-grade idiots like Steven Colbert/failed actor Alec Baldwin are not like patriotic actors back when.

CULTURE CLASH BASHED

Creeps like Colbert were tearing down family and culture but fortunately their ratings slipped below par.

Not only are primitives seen as more noble, also children being untainted from culture, tho' trouble.

Confused daycare Millennials idiotically fighting for Geo Soro's New World Order yet they don't know.

Emmy's: The talentless low IQ drug addicted puppets caused such a backlash they're out of luck.

HOW DARE YOU ADORE THEM

It's insane, for Hollywood adoration you should feel ashamed. Specious arguments, I get bored with same.

Jane Fonda hated America then, hates America now—another sick witch seeing herself as highbrow.

As long as your art's about social justice, God's not coming through and the same for any false premise.

A "sexist lying hypocritical egotistical bigot" the stupid witch called Trump the prosperity-spigot.

Feminist say men (and Antifa says whites) are doing things they are not—carelessly they cause riots.

Stop saying men touch "inappropriately"--its the Muslims but you conflate and it's dangerous/silly.

You want to make it look men are bad cuz that's your gig and it's so incendiary saying men are cads.

They get along fine then she sees a feminist friend and turns on husband, going way over the line.

White men just wanna live their lives and be left alone. Stop blaming--you're not an artist but a clone.

CULTURE CLASH BASHED

You need a subject so find the closet outlet: leftists are maggots when it comes to that, braggin'

If anything white men are scared of women--the feminists are meaner after talking with their friends.

To make money they turn to trendy topics of scapegoating innocent people/it's really quite evil.

Cuz they hated men they all wanted Hillary who woulda flooded them with misogynists who would kill em.

THERE'S MEN AND WOMEN, DOGS AND CATS

There's men and women, dogs and cats, sun and moon. We can see things the liberal way or with wisdom.

You can't dispute these false accusations cuz it's all anecdotal that whites are racist or men claw women.

Instead of using trendy topics why not learn something, take time to mature, you're just a novice.

It's so embarrassing how they virtue signal on trendy topics then expect us to buy it like we're twits.

Dumbed lemmings will believe ridiculous notions of a social hypnotic just cuz the others believe it.

It's not about reason but a bunch of lemmings jumping off a cliff: truth is what the group says it is.

It's a lonely cold atmosphere adapting to liberals cuz it's all about the social and other drivel.
For my friends everything, for my enemies the law. Oscar Benavides

Homes breaking up over Trump. It comes down to what news do they watch: truth or made up.

The danger they cause: Men are afraid of women who get meaner after talking to the girls (blah-blah).

CULTURE CLASH BASHED

They brought themselves to their newest, deepest low. Arrogance blinds them but we see/know.

Could've been in the White House ya know, but Hillary's signing copies of her fiction book at Costco.

If the ugly Emmy's don't push you away from liberalism it means you are just too far gone.

The American tragedy: millionaires speaking on how they are an oppressed minority/need sympathy.

RAPPERS BASH TRUMP

Rappers bash trump to revive their faltering careers but since they stooped so low we kicked em all downstairs.

Stupid Bow Wow and uncle ruined careers forever cuz they went so low.

In obscure loser (washed up rapper) news, Bow Wow is back.

You act cool in a little boy's world saying kidnapping wives for sex slavery is good but it's over for you, hood.

BowWow sass: some day the good Lord will visit you with justice.

Only the dumbest buy liberal lies but fake news the clear despise.

The last refuge of tyrants is war when they're hanging on by their fingernails.

She wasn't social but had the feminist influence: divorce is good, men are bad. She was wrong, he wasn't a cad.

What is an ugly old bag? An older female who doesn't educate youth on morals but is a dirty thief herself.

He's very "nice" as he ruins his country. ALL liberals with out fail are virtue signalers and it makes money.

Violent threats against the president are now ok?

CULTURE CLASH BASHED

Everything they do turns to crap and blows up in their face but they don't care--they're moving forward.

WRONGSPEAK = OSTRACIZED FROM SOCIETY

You say something wrong and you're removed from society never to be heard from again: family and friends.

The people have not been in charge for so long we've forgotten what it was like and everything's verboten.

I just wanna be with patriots: the right-wingers and bitter clingers.

Tell em "this is immature--virtue signaling to a trendy topic."

Adapting to liberal idiots caused insanity/decades lost, but it's like being in jail: it built character/I'm the best.

No more situational ethics, "going with the flow" or "historical evolution" (legislating the courts by politicians).

Millennials the most servile, brainwashed, evil creatures you can imagine but gen. Z is opposite/can be friends.

He's used to getting things his way ("you're fired"). Worried about his emotions with this/getting too tired.

The Art of the Deal is not working with a crippled, social warrior, obstructive and bought off government.

It's a corrupt evil communist government.

Why aren't filthy dirty rap stars thrown into jail? We want justice, we're sick of it and fear USA is failed.

Just look at the trashy broken streets of a decaying degenerate municipality ruled by corrupt liberals.

Truth is opposite to appearances, based not on what everyone thinks (herd view) but on facts and sciences.

CULTURE CLASH BASHED

ALL advancing their own career so true leaders watch out who whispers in their ear, learned from Caesar.

Skilled dealmaker unwilling to strike compromises blew up. How to get other things done? Get rid of Brutus Ryan

Different groups commit different crimes and that's not a racial slur it's cold hard reality/the new paradigm.

Some are 6X more likely to rob, some twice as likely to murder but liberals say "we're all the same", oh brother.

STATISTICS ON GROUPS AND THEIR CRIMES

Stats on groups and their crimes don't say why it is, just that it is.

Academics plot against each other, undermine. Backbite, connive to advance over like bureaucrat guys.

Stop your blanket accusation of "men". Women had it made with western white men but you conflate again.

Big cities are a threat to the health, the wealth and the liberty of mankind. Thomas Jefferson

Defeat political correctness, secure borders, explode stocks, arrest pedophiles and defund sanctuary cities.

Love of liberty, freedom and ideas unites us--not skin color--but the social engineers don't want that, it's war.

They just wanna feel they're part of a successful group (not be part of real freedom/prosperity) so stay duped.

Progressives are the new Puritans: joyless and authoritarian.

Justice warrioring degrades your art and holds you back. Stop conforming and be a true artist not a sad sack.

Left thought they had cornered "cool"--can't imagine the right could be the new counter-culture to rule.

CULTURE CLASH BASHED

Census will now ask gender identity.

You can put a sheep with a lion but only one's coming out in the morning.

Problem with appeasement: you get weaker and the enemy stronger.

Liberalism stinks yet it's been a cultural worldview for decades, making decisions and saying what to think.

Universities are now stealing all resources from American students and giving them to illegal truants.

FEMINISTS CONFLATE LIKE IT'S "ALL" MEN

Feminists conflate like "all" men rape but are unconcerned for the female victims of the Muslim faith.

The biggest enemy of women is women, and that ignorance is a catastrophe.

Feminist: lies about the wage gap, lies about campus rape culture, stop.

Electricity from Clean Coal costs 25 % of the cost of natural gas and 1/6 of the cost of windmills/solar panels.

So long as crap is filtered through the lens of social justice and identity politics for a start, it's considered "art".

Conceptual art has profound thinking behind it. But the current junk-shop art of ordinary things--forget it.

If people say it's "art" it's "art" even though it's rubbish. These are conformists not dissidents producing trash.

You can't ever please the permanently offended "identitarians".

Modern art is a physical manifestation born of the demented minds of social justice warriors. Paul Joseph Watson

They think that tingle is giving them power but it's just sucking them down, soured

CULTURE CLASH BASHED

I see no conflict between being powerful and feminine but liberals do, the fools.

Making a cultural dent is a turkey shoot cuz they're SO dumbed down: pursue!

Your enemy splits off then rises up against you and then he gets his whole tribe to do it too.

Trump refused to shake the dirty culprit's hand like the other politicians-- that proved who he was, again.

Adverse possession (squatting) succeeds. 120 days to evict and other regulatory obstructions and proceeds.

MANIPULATORS WITH THEIR OWN AGENDAS

Manipulators with their own agendas, that's the mainstream news in America.

He knows 15 moves ahead where everyone's going so we get mad at him then later see his game plan.

Justice warrioring degrades your art and hold you back. Stop conforming and be a true artist not a sad sack.

Obama was the reason sun shined and birds sang (while nation can hang) yet Trump over-delivers and it boomerangs.

Tell em "this is immature--virtue signaling on a trendy topic."

So Obama insider "Gibbs" was behind the MacDonald Trash-Trump Tweet. Good sleuthing now it's all complete.

I was so sweet til they got ahold of me. Got no friends cuz they read the papers and idiots won't be seen with me.

The major reaction of the wife of the alcoholic is to get drunk herself, then they blame her more, repelled.

Libs continue to pound that Hillary won, as if our founders ever wanted rule by a mob.

CULTURE CLASH BASHED

We elected someone to clean it up and he's doing it--looking up!

Fascism came to America under the guise of liberalism: total control/no freedom.

After Hillary Clinton, Maxine Waters and many other feminists people might disdain having women in office.

They don't care about Benghazi, Kidafi, Haiti or Pizzagate (etc. etc. etc.) they just love Hillary.

IDENTITY POLITICS AND VIRTUE SIGNALING

Virtue signaling/identity politics: a fraud but women suck it up to be mod.

Here's the same old divide, women. Only one solution, don't talk to em.

Unable to see their faults they assume it's prejudice against women. Their own denial blinds them, again.

There is right and wrong. Absolute morality, not relativism of the throng.

That's not killing it's defending against an aggressor coming against you or it's an unjust war/sinning.

It's so scary how much women love Hillary not caring what she's done whether Kadafi, Haiti or Benghazi.

Hillary could get in if enough dumb women or wimpy feminist men.

Weak leaders have paralysis in fear of retaliation.

If the church doesn't talk of sin they're just social hall religion, a need to be seen and so incredibly boring!

All wars began with a false flag to gin up support. WWII killed 50 million and the left wants nuclear--come Lord!

A Christian holiday. How wholesome, how sweet, a rare treat, a meaningful revival to ruminate about and tweet.

CULTURE CLASH BASHED

Truth is the opposite to appearances, based not on what everyone thinks (herd view) but on facts and sciences.

Juan and Geraldo are boring, liberal, aggravating speedbumps yet they're on FOX constantly. Yuk.

Why would Assad wanna kill his own people? He's a crazy man in a country filled with factions, many evil.

Conservative = textualist, by the book.

No analysis of Hillary allowed: Benghazi, emails, Libya were just pseudo-scandals, stuff made up, fowl.

THEY CRY WHEN ARCHETYPES DIE

Why they cry? Because their savior, light itself, Athena was extinguished: archetype, demolished.

If they assimilate it's different but if they don't they're "citizens", right? Liberals don't care about our life.

Liberal family members are always offended. That's their whole thing when coming against the splendid.

About Trump: Give him a chance, watch close and wish well. Cheer what's sound, criticize what isn't and tell.

What to tell your scared kids: the left did this, demonizing Mr. Trump and making him monstrous.

The left is irate over it's own false narrative.

After getting news focus on inner peace or die--for "men's hearts will fail them" from fear or media lies.

"I hate your network, everyone at CNN is a liar and you should be ashamed." Trump To CNN executives today.

All this race-baiting garbage isn't working anymore.

CULTURE CLASH BASHED

I'm sick of this so go ahead and appoint the backstabber Romney. He's gonna bite you cuz he's a phony.

Trump: He called you a phony and a fraud and you pick him from all those truly loving this country and God?

Many thanksgiving family fights, all cuz they watched different news at night.

On Hillary: Trump doesn't want to take the time--it's low priority compared to saving the country.

Mass divorces occurring over politics. A wider divide, they can't stand each other, choose to quit and split.

Megyn Kelly says Trump-lovers "stink" in Hollywood and just her saying that made me hate the broad.

POLITICAL PARADOXES

The extent to which he is needed is measured by the extent to which they hate/try to impeach him.

Even though he's making things better for them they still wanna kill him cuz they're parasites in bedlam.

Since everyone's the same "if one group does better it's because they stole it", so target and kill it.

We're in the fight and that's most of the battle. Alex Jones

They call themselves "democrats" but are the least democratic when letting go of power: low class rats.

Rightists are being disinvited to family dinners. Thank the Lord you've escaped fate/become a winner.

I don't wish them any harm but they wish me harm. I will fight back as should any American when alarmed.

They don't give to charity, they just virtue signal. They aren't true liberals, it's something else I don't wanna know.

CULTURE CLASH BASHED

I am consumed by the animating contest of liberty. I do nothing else cuz it's about survival itself, believe me.

He's backing off on climate hoax/giving Hillary hopes as a charm offensive? We need to pray, folks.

He's willing to retreat from strong positions expressed in the most strident tones--are we being thrown bones?

Would you have approved of this behavior in the fifties or is this just social hebephrenia from the lefties?

Done with politics. Who needs all these flip-flops, fake rights and all their other frustrating/unnerving antics?

I suppose it'll come out all right in the end, we can only hope that Trump (the genius) will remain our friend.

Maybe Trump's a genius faking us all out. Let's not micromanage just pray he does right and has clout.

I DON'T LIKE LIBERALS: GO TO THE DEVIL

I don't like liberals, I find them disgusting and cruel. Is this how you feel too?

Election exhaustion is putting people in mental hospitals and now they're getting drunk over Trump.

In that world you pay them off so they won't kill you like the Mafia too.

The right was upset with Trump but if he had Obama would've pardoned her. Relax, it's not over.

Voters, listen: Many donate to the Clintons to stave off aggression--an appeasement posture of men.

That you can't see through Hillary Clinton is a real obstruction cuz what does it say about your perception?

Hillary Clinton is a notorious criminal too but like pooh on the shoe you just won't go away will you.

CULTURE CLASH BASHED

Genius Trump told us he doesn't say what he's gonna do. Relax, he'll do what he said for you and me too.

Folks just don't wanna be happy. No gathering around with family, only whining about past centuries.

Let the new attorney general go after Hillary. He will, but for our president it's just a matter of priorities.

Now we see who's stupid enough to go along with these things. It's a great relief, actually--truly seeing.

The Krazy Kollege Kids want all drugs legalized. They don't want the wall to keep em out—are you surprised?

GO FORWARD—DON'T LOOK BACKWARD

To go forward, don't look backward. It's a waste of time despite the many holding you in line.

Good riddance California, we'll be blessed: rid of the karma from your debaucheries/liberal sickness.

A dinner guest started railing about history. What a witch she ruined our nice dinner so rudely/totally.

She was home from college and how she had changed: a whiney arrogant student had became deranged.

She acts so superior over her lofty ideals but no one cares how she feels, just shut up--you have NO appeal!

She wanted the limelight at dinner as if she were superior--then she said we're all equal except us, the inferior.

She said "I'll celebrate when the victims declare victory", so why did she come--just to give us her story?

In her smugness she couldn't stand normal conversation, she had to divert it all to her, a boring aberration.

CULTURE CLASH BASHED

Good news: Obummer stripped of power till Donald gets in, the true man of the hour and high as a tower.

You say the KKK (Krazy Kollege Kids) aren't prejudiced? BS! They are the worst thing of all: ageists.

She was Ms. Superior through the whole family dinner and I wonder how many experienced similar?

Social justice warriors: I'm afraid of em. Cuza what happened to Indians she'd like to kill us, ex-friends.

All through dinner it was about the poor Indians but by her deep cleavage she wanted to be noticed as woman.

YOU'RE THE BEST DESPITE THE POLLS

Be you despite polls. Play a role, lose your soul.

Don't worry about Trump It's just a fake to the left to hold off aggression until his time has come.

The spirit of oppression is beginning to lift and rays of sunlight are coming through the clouds: God's gift!

They wanna be the only ones with the spirit of creativity. They control it all, like chopping down a tree.

They project their disgusting perverted lifestyle by accusing him of what they do and it's really totally vile.

Our win has triggered the left's exponential obstructions, riot accelerations and simply made up deceptions.

God gave us an imperfect servant like King David to take down Goliath.

The great awards like the Nobel Peace prize given to warmongers are the biggest joke of those in power.

Knowing the enemy is half the battle. Lord takes care of the rest: He puts one down and the other in a castle.

CULTURE CLASH BASHED

I believe in conservation but progressives use environmentalism to push the Marxist agenda. Michael Savage

Just the fact your wife loves Hillary is reason to question your sanity for adapting to liberal reality.

Turn from all your fake, dumbed, attention-driven friends who love Hillary cuz that's the sign, really.

People are so dumbed it's all name-recognition with Hillary Clinton--their past without rememberin'.

SELLING SOULS FOR A SLICE

They sell their souls to get their slice.

When Civics was removed the commies made their move.

Riots will just remind us of the vulgar ideology we rejected when voting for Trump. Paul Joseph Watson

It is certain that ignorance allied with power is the most ferocious enemy justice can have. James A. Baldwin

From false religion many horrible things stem. That's just the way it is and thus the importance of true doctrine.

NWO/liberals are aligned against Christianity, sovereign states, traditional morals and the family. Vladimir Putin

Without Christian moral roots we become brutes.

All laws which are repugnant to the constitution are null and void. Marbury vs. Madison 1803

Tyrants take over by degree as the system tests the public to see (how much we want to be free).

They're gonna roll it out by saying the camps/gungrabs/tyranny are to save and safeguard society. Alex Jones

CULTURE CLASH BASHED

The NDAA: a blight. They wanna ram things through so we silently go into the long, disastrous black night.

It's God, people aren't that important—sorry

Regulations kill jobs and bloat government.

Need a businessman who's gonna cut dead weight: can't wait!

The worst president in history: We're all outa hope and most have no change, sorry.

WE DON'T NEED THE COOL

We need foreign policy nerds in office not "cool" people who are novice.

Imagine if the "horrible alt right" had thrown feces at Obama--we'd never stop hearing about it, America.

Victimhood culture is lucrative.

It's a meritocracy now—no more victimhood status. Goodbye communists, race-baiters and mentally ill artists.

They hate freedom and meritocracy, they wanna ride the wave of lucrative victimhood and utter hypocrisy.

Facts: Trump's already doing so much for blacks but still the left calls him a racist and gives him the axe.

Anarchists, anti-capitalists and collectivists have had their way for 8 long years of terror and horrible accidents.

Trump is a return to law and order, a threat to the mob of social justice warriors.

Increasingly, lewd leftists will stand out and look disgusting as they pout.

Ideas are bullet-proof: no army can stop an idea whose time has come.

CULTURE CLASH BASHED

Feminism is a mean, vindictive, spiteful, nasty man-hating philosophy with little to do with equality. Milo

A look into homes shows what happens when we let standards slide. Throw things wherever and there they lie.

Did they call you a clown, a loser or a liar? No worries they said the same about our president, a ball of fire.

I'm sickened by how protestors are throwin feces and urine. They should be jailed and defunded--are you in?

ALL IMBECILES CALL US RACIST

After years attacked as sexist, racist, xenophobic, homophobic and deplorable we're free of imbeciles.

Protestors are silly pawns cued by globalists. Undeveloped intellectually they can't think outa the box.

Likes/fans/favs don't reflect truth.

I love the POTUS! To hell with the naive children who protest.

All mafia are "nice" before the stab in the back. Don't worry, he'll get him/her--he's got that knack.

What they call a "dark speech" we call refreshing truth and a great relief.

Liberals call his speech "Hitlerian" cuz he wants to put us first--aren't they ridiculous, everything's reversed.

It's a dialectic: We needed Obama to get Trump. The pendulum swung back and now we've over the hump.

The minute Obama got on the chopper I felt such relief: Like two tons off my shoulder, fell into a deep sleep.

Trump's not just a savior of America but all Western culture. We're dwindling while east is multiplying, for sure.

CULTURE CLASH BASHED

Exchanged local garb for herringbone, that was cool and chic--put down bitter clingers as if they were the creeps.

Liberals defined by beliefs: take our guns while opening the borders despite our pleas, sanctuary cities.

It's probably true that obscene exhibitionism

I don't care what they know or say about conservatism, if indecent they're just another bum.

Despite being veiled by nice image, evil comes out in spots and to the prudent these are good shocks.

WIMPS CONTROLLED BY GROUPTHINK

If controlled by groupthink, you're a wimp. This adaptation makes men cower and dumb women primp.

Doublethink says all things are true and simultaneously banishes anyone disagreeing with that view.

Newspeak says my actions define who I am and if you object you're a hater and that's the whole story, amen.

"Offensive speech" on campus (says the crazy liberal view) are called haters, racists and bigots too.

Liberals are fakers: No original thought whatsoever and very disrespectful of thinkers.

They think they're smart due to "elite" schools but due to liberalism they're dumb/not truly cool.

So-called "altruism" is actually collectivism which is the worst kind of tyranny preventing optimism.

They know they're wrong: To cover that up they act more that way, confirmed by the throng.

The sin of the century is the loss of the sense of sin. Increasingly each day we are a trash bin.

"Don't tell me you're good, only God is good". That's what Jesus said to those with hearts of wood.

They preach "tolerance" but are only tolerant of those who agree with them. Liberal thinking: condemn.

They're not truly dumb just brainwashed not to want freedom--they label that as slavery, in sum.

DISCERN GOD'S TIMING: GO OR STAY

You need to know when to stop and when to go. Get outa there, man--what do these people know?

Trendies: power trips of arrogance and narcissism, If you disagree they accuse you of racism.

When a leader is surrounded by a spirit of familiarity, it's easy to lose clarity from this hostile polarity.

It's just a herd. Conformists are not the True Self, it's all words and superficial and silly is preferred.

They're very clever: they wanna control it all with robotic levers so all loving ties are severed.

They say they're bringing lightness but really it's dark. The new illuminati: the trendies are sharks.

These people are sick. And they can be violent when just a little offended--yet thick as bricks, hicks.

People are socially needy cuz they've been told by the social culture that being alone is creepy.

They care more about that he offends than that he tells the truth--a social generation, the uncouth.

CULTURE CLASH BASHED

I don't care what they say about Trump, he rings our bell--others too if they're intellectual.

A dumbed down public is allowing this to happen. This was a longterm plan instilled like fashion.

Liberals can't face facts–it's all politically correct reality (women, blacks) giving us the axe.

We've so taken freedom for granted. When liberty is lost all goes to hell unless God has repented.

You're thinking these notions are yours? No, you've been programmed by the mind control corps.

RECAP THOUGHTS ON LIES WE BOUGHT

Who dresses in white? Phonies, democrats and the KKK (blights).

The time has come for a new program of national rebuilding. Donald Trump

They're master spinsters, that's what they do.

It's the style to hate Trump and it's getting old. Public fools, so bold.

They'll eat their words soon, when their finances improve.

So Presidential, so Romanesque, so statesmanly–our guy's the best.

Just shut up. We won and you didn't.

It's only been a few months and he's delivering—blast off, man!

We'll see the end of Hillary and we'll soon see the end of Soros. Alex Jones

Kids fail in school cuz the school failed them.

Republicans may be horrible but the democrats are a special type of trash. AJ

A shot in the arm for female entrepreneurs and dems are still disdainful/weird?

CULTURE CLASH BASHED

Not naming the enemy leads to it's expansion.

The time for small thinking is over. Trump will prevail over dem posers.

She thinks it's all her. Even after she copied you she's the star: ignore.

Modern liberal pop Satanism: self-centered people and perversion.

Abortion, a mistake, you're forgiven. But left sees it as a ritual they're lovin'

Power grasping pretty boy Paul Ryan is always blocking and lyin'

With each speech Trump's raising up the spirit of America--pride, hurrah

You must raise the morale of a citizenry for them to act properly.

He's got broad shoulders, a big heart but is willing to fight. Mike Pence

See the renewal, feel the renewal: America's coming back again, new.

We must be unified to build a culture and the dems are splitting: closure.

Since man has a fallen nature we're careful who's in power, for sure.

Stock market up 3.9 trillion since Trump

Save yourself ten hours a day, just catch Hannity

Those who the Gods would destroy they would first make mad. Prometheus

A Christian nation with principals astounding in their ability to protect personal freedom.

Violent misogyny is their central point.

There's a reason you don't wanna turn on FOX anymore--go with that.

It doesn't matter if kids know all 50 states--they just gotta know all 57 genders.

Preaching against sin is "hate speech".

CULTURE CLASH BASHED

Feminism: an excuse to treat men like crap. Milo

Political correctness promotes pedophilia.

Jail BowWow and uncle.

Trump a horrible racist? How ridiculous!

They undermined him, set him up for a fall, his own advisors that's all.

Truth is alive and lives@Infowars, lies and elitism fight for their lives@Time.

Communism is based on the false dream of utopia so no need for prayer.

Obsession with the environment is a false conscience after God's rejected.

Delete the news, have found time! Update with Hannity, Jones, Savage, Trump.

Sin is a mal-adaptive coping device (to deal with anxiety) once enticed.

Christian Psychology: Repent of sin, symptoms leave.

The dumb dump on Trump.

When the church signed the gag order they signed for judgment.

The churches wanted tax exempt status so bad they gladly self-censored.

Reject the hex from these leftist wrecks.

KAREN KELLOCK PH.D.

M.S. Political Science, San Diego State. Ph.D. in Psychology, University of California Irvine. Postdoctoral: UCI School of Medicine, Dept. of Psychiatry [NIMH Grants]. Developed the Debris Theory of Disease, a theory of system pathology in 120 books and 22 textbooks for the general public. The theory has a general formula: All disease is obstruction, all recovery is elimination, all success is attraction. The three obstructions are people, habit and food. Remove obstruction and snap to your goals, waiting in the wings.